the quick-start guide to your first property

the quick-start guide to your first property

PICK UP YOUR KEYS

simpler, smarter & sooner

GLEN JAMES & RACHELLE KROON

WILEY

First published 2026 by John Wiley & Sons Australia, Ltd

ISBN: 978-1-394-41460-4

A catalogue record for this book is available from the National Library of Australia

Registered Office
John Wiley & Sons Australia, Ltd. Level 4, 600 Bourke Street, Melbourne, VIC 3000, Australia

For details of our global editorial offices, customer services, and more information about Wiley products visit us at www.wiley.com.

Wiley also publishes its books in a variety of electronic formats and by print-on-demand. Some content that appears in standard print versions of this book may not be available in other formats.

Cover design by Wiley

Photo of Glen and Rach by Grapefruit Creative

Suburban house photo (p299): © Elias Bitar / Adobe Stock

Cover design concept by Jason Knight www.askjasonknight.com

Set in 10/16pt and Tisa Pro by Straive, Chennai, India.

Printed and bound by CPI Group (UK) Ltd, Croydon, CR0 4YY

C9781394414604_160626

The manufacturer's authorized representative according to the EU General Product Safety Regulation is Wiley-VCH GmbH, Boschstr. 12, 69469 Weinheim, Germany, e-mail: Product_Safety@wiley.com.

Contents

Hi and welcome home!

You may have heard people say the Australian property market is cooked. So what does that mean if you want to buy your first property, either as a first home to live in or an investment property? It's important to understand our current climate. You know it feels expensive to buy a property — but it's not just a feeling, it's fact. If we look at the numbers, they're staggering (see table 1).

Table 1: median house prices in 1990 vs 2025

Year	Median house price in Australia	Median household income in Australia	Direct multiple required to buy a home
1990	~$144 000	~$32 770	~4.39×
2025	~$848 858	~$92 040	~9.22×

Data compiled from ABS Average Weekly Earnings (1990, 2024), ABS Census Insights: Income in Australia (2024), Cotality Home Value Index (Aug. 2025) and Abelson & Chung, House Prices in Australia: 1970–2003 (Economic Record, 2005).

This is a very high-level look at what's going on. If you dig deeper into the data, homes in the 1990s were probably closer to three times the average household income. We're not going to unpack all the structural stuff here: things like wages, government policies, supply and demand, or labour shortages. But we want you to know buying property really is harder than it used to be and if it feels tough, you're not imagining it.

The intent isn't to scare you because there are things you can control. These are your own goals, strategy, lifestyle and income. Rest assured, while we see numbers like those in table 1, and record housing prices for capital cities, there are hundreds of property markets in Australia. The market that matters to you isn't the 'property market' itself—it's the location where you want to buy and the type of dwelling you're after. If the big data says the median price for a home in a capital city is well over $1 million, this is irrelevant if you're after a two-bedroom townhouse two hours away from the capital city that's worth less than $1 million.

Is it hard out there right now? Yes. Is it easy to get discouraged and not take action? Yes. Is it impossible to get your first property? No. It might just take some different thinking, some strategy, some risk and a team of people to guide you.

You're not alone

We asked the *money money money* and *this is property* podcast communities what they wanted in a book about buying your first property—and that's how this book came about. We are the first team members in your journey and we are here to help.

This book was created to answer one question: what do first-time buyers wish they'd known before starting their property journey?

A word from Rach

My goal is to encourage younger Australians, particularly those who believe home ownership may not be achievable. I want to educate and inspire, help with your goals, open your eyes to some different pathways and assist with 'getting you in'.

The world has changed and the old rules don't really apply anymore. Getting into property today requires new thinking and different strategies. My goal is to help people get in earlier where they can and also to help those who bought years ago understand just how tough it is for younger generations trying to break in now — and how much harder it's likely to get.

So many people have come to us for advice and wished they had reached out sooner. I believe our education system should include subjects like how to buy a property. I'd love people to read this book while they are studying or when they first start working so they can set a goal for when they enter the property market and to be informed about how others like them have done it.

Read this book to get started, then pop it on your bookshelf to refer to when you get closer to buying your first property.

I was lucky enough to have conversations about property growing up. I entered the market early and have never looked back. It was my path to financial freedom and is why I have been able to make bold choices later in life. My property portfolio gave me the confidence to leave my corporate role to start a business. Security gave me that luxury of choice. I am not selling a get-rich-quick scheme or promising 30 properties before 30 is achievable in today's world. I would like to encourage as many people as I can to enter the property market and to offer as much practical advice as I can for people who are planning and preparing and for those who have already started the process.

I am a millennial, an elder millennial. We were the 'generation now' and were criticised for lack of patience. In relation to property, we supposedly lacked the grit to go without to save for a home deposit. It was infuriating for me to hear my parents talk this way because my father was able to buy multiple investment properties on one very average income. That was impossible for me and if you are a Gen Z feeling the same way, I get it. It may be harder for you than it was for me, but I want to encourage you.

One big fact remains true. Getting into the Australian property market early matters because property in Australia has historically been one of the most reliable and powerful ways to build long-term wealth, stability and financial security and the benefits are greater the earlier you start (no pressure).

Along with my own property journey, I have been privileged to share the property journeys of thousands of clients buying homes and investment properties. I hope to share as many stories with you as I can to illustrate practically how people are entering the property market and to share the wins and losses along the way.

I won't be sharing stories about Gen X clients who are multiple investors and how they built wealth quickly and leveraged their property gains over decades. The stories in this book will be of recent first-home buyers and first-time investors: how they entered the market and the tools they used, as well as many practical tips about the overall buying journey.

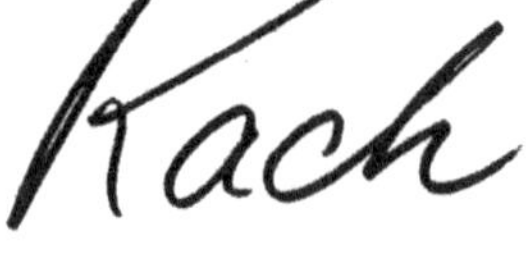

A word from Glen

I was in two minds about writing this book. I have what you could call a love–hate relationship with property. If you have been listening to my *money money money* podcast for a while, you will know I flip and flop every other week about it. On one hand, property is a powerful way to build wealth. On the other, the current prices across Australia make me feel flat for the people who are still trying to get a foot in the door.

After plenty of chats with Rach, we decided to put this book together because we both believe it is still possible to buy your first home. It might not be where you live right now, but there are still affordable entry points around the country. If you are willing to think differently and plan carefully, you can get there.

After years of talking with podcast listeners, meeting people at live events and hearing stories in our community, I have seen that ordinary Australians are still managing to buy property without big incomes or family help. The ones who do it share a few key traits.

First, they are intentional. Buying their first home is not just another thing on a long list of goals. It is *the* goal. They are not trying to save for Europe, a wedding, a new car and a house all at once. Every dollar has a job, and the job is to save for a property.

Second, most of them don't have car loans. They are often driving something modest that they own outright. It's not that you can't buy a property if you have car repayments, but I rarely see it. They also stay clear of consumer debt such as credit cards, buy-now-pay-later schemes and personal loans. This makes a huge difference when it comes to getting a home loan approved. Not only from a mortgage servicing point of view but for freeing up cash flow and ensuring they're not spending more than they earn.

Third, they are patient and know it takes time. For many, it's a three- or four-year journey. But that time will pass, and those who start early are always grateful they did. The trick is to understand your strategy now and make steady progress. Small, consistent steps beat big, inconsistent ones.

I'm amazed by how many people don't use the First Home Super Saver (FHSS) scheme when wanting to buy their first home to live in. It's one of the few legal hacks that can save you thousands in tax and speed up saving your deposit. Part of the reason Rach and I wrote this book is to help you spot opportunities like this incentive and actually use them.

Before you dive into the chapters ahead, I want you to know this. This book is not about hype. It is about giving you a clear, practical path and the encouragement to start walking it. If you have felt disheartened—like worrying that the system is rigged or it's all too hard—this book is for you. You can do this and we'll show you how.

Let's get into it.

The journey to your first property

Buying a first property is often described as a rite of passage — and it may not be a linear path as it was for previous generations (see figure 1). For many Australians, it represents independence, stability and the promise of future wealth. It's the biggest purchase most people will ever make, yet it's also one of the least understood.

For previous generations, buying a home was almost straightforward: work hard, save consistently and when you had a deposit, head to the bank and choose from a small selection of houses in your local area. Today, the picture is far more complex. Rising property prices, stricter lending rules and a crowded market have created a landscape that feels overwhelming, especially for first-time buyers.

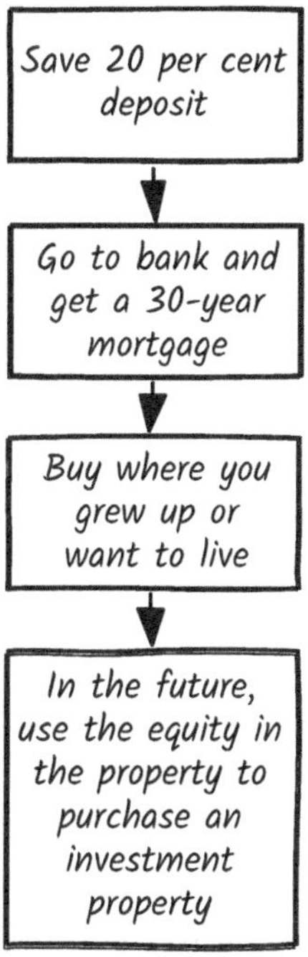

The path to your first home probably won't be a straight line to a 'forever' home, and that's completely normal. Most first-home buyers now take a few unexpected steps along the way. Maybe you've always imagined buying your dream home first, but your starting point ends up being an investment property that helps you build the equity to get there. Or maybe you've been gearing up for years of scrimping and saving a deposit, only to realise a parental guarantee could fast-track the whole thing.

Figure 1: previous generations could use a very straight-forward linear process

This is where education, good advice and an open mindset become your superpowers. Buying property is emotional — of course it is — but your first step might not look like the final picture in your head. And that's okay. Stay flexible, stay curious and remember that a different path can still lead you exactly where you want to go.

Over months of surveys, conversations and interviews with people across Australia, six themes emerged repeatedly. These weren't small, isolated issues — they were consistent pressure points that caused confusion, fear and at times, regret. These six themes (outlined below) form the foundation of this book.

The goal is simple: by exploring each theme in depth, you'll have a clear plan for navigating your journey. Whether your first property is a home to live in or an investment, this book provides the clarity and confidence that so many buyers say they wish they'd had from the start.

1 Your 'why' + choosing a strategy

We'll start by talking about your 'why': why are you buying a property? This is key and narrows in on what your goal is. From this foundation we can dig into the strategies that support achieving that goal.

Some people purchase a property to live in, while others choose to buy an investment first and continue renting elsewhere. Each approach has its own challenges and opportunities. Government grants and concessions generally apply only to owner-occupied homes. Tax rules differ between investments and principal places of residence. Even the type of property that makes a strong investment may not suit someone's day-to-day lifestyle.

There is also a third path that sits in the middle and it is one many buyers take without realising it has a name. You may buy a property to live in initially, maximise first-home buyer concessions and state-based incentives, then move out later and turn that property into a rental as your circumstances change. This can be a very strategic move, using the rules as they are designed while building long-term wealth. The key is understanding the implications upfront so the transition is planned, not reactive.

To unpack this, in chapters 1, 4, 5, 6 and 7 we will look at:

- financial advantages and disadvantages
- eligibility for grants and government programs
- lifestyle flexibility and long-term planning
- the risks of trying to do everything at once.

With clear guidance, you can choose a path that aligns with both your personal life and your broader wealth strategy.

2 Saving for a deposit and grants

Saving a deposit remains a significant challenge for many people. The traditional advice of saving 20 per cent of the purchase price is daunting, especially in high-cost areas. Fortunately, there are ways to accelerate progress. The Australian Government 5% Deposit Scheme, parental guarantees, the First Home Super Saver (FHSS) scheme and other incentives and strategies may help you get a place sooner. State-based grants and stamp duty concessions can also reduce the required savings target, but only if buyers know how to access them.

In chapters 2, 3 and 4, we will give you strategies for:

- setting realistic savings goals
- choosing the right savings accounts and offset accounts
- understanding how government incentives work
- deciding whether to buy sooner with a smaller deposit or wait longer.

With the right information, you can shorten your timeline and reduce the stress of saving.

3 Mortgage and borrowing concerns

For many buyers, the first challenge isn't finding the perfect home—it's understanding how much they can afford to borrow. Mortgages are the foundation of most property purchases, but they're also one of the most intimidating parts of the process. The lending world is filled with confusing terms: serviceability, loan-to-value ratio, offset accounts, fixed and variable rates and interest-only loans, to name a few. For someone encountering these terms for the first time, it can feel like learning a foreign language.

The problem isn't just the language; it's the complexity of the system itself. Lenders assess borrowers using strict criteria that vary between banks and can change at any time. A person who's pre-approved today may find that approval withdrawn tomorrow because of a small change in income, a new bank rule or even adjustments to how lenders calculate risk.

Many first-home buyers start house hunting without clearly understanding their borrowing capacity. They attend inspections, fall in love with a property, then discover they can't secure the finance they need. This creates disappointment, wasted time and sometimes leads to rushed or poor decisions.

Mortgage brokers can be valuable allies in this process. They help borrowers compare multiple lenders, explain different loan options and guide them through complex paperwork.

Understanding the mortgage process early can save stress, money and heartache. Chapters 2 and 3 will help you understand the process and equip you to:

- calculate realistic borrowing capacity
- compare lenders and loan products effectively

- understand how brokers work and the value they bring
- build a financial buffer to prevent future hardships.

The aim isn't just to secure a mortgage, but to secure the right mortgage that fits your long-term goals and offers flexibility as life changes.

4 Understanding the buying process

Even with finance and negotiation strategies in place, many buyers still feel overwhelmed by the process itself. Buying a property can and does involve many players: lenders, mortgage brokers, real estate agents, buyer's agents, conveyancers, solicitors, building inspectors, government offices and others. Each step has deadlines and specific tasks (see figure 2). Without guidance, it can feel like navigating a maze without a map.

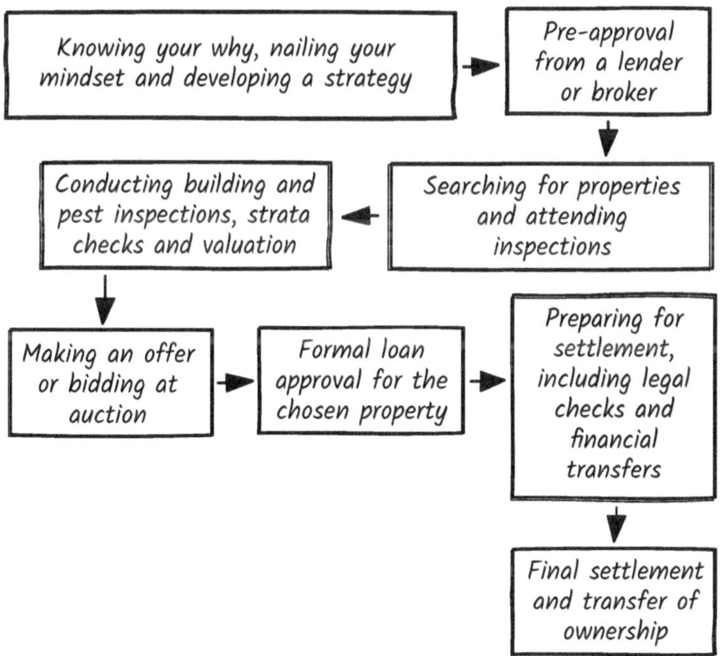

Figure 2: the typical buying processes

Mistakes can occur at any stage. Missing a deadline may delay settlement. Misunderstanding a contract clause could create legal problems. Rushing an inspection might result in buying a property with hidden defects.

In chapters 8 and 9, we will break down each stage in simple language. You will learn who's responsible for each task, when it needs to be done and how to confirm nothing's been overlooked. The aim is to replace confusion with a clear roadmap from start to finish.

5 Dealing with agents and contracts

Once financing becomes clear and is secured, another challenge appears: dealing with real estate agents and contracts. Real estate agents are skilled professionals whose responsibility is to achieve the best possible outcome for the seller, not the buyer. This creates an immediate imbalance. First-home buyers, often inexperienced and emotionally invested, risk being out-negotiated before they even realise a negotiation has begun.

Many buyers describe feeling pressured during inspections or private sales. Agents may mention other interested parties, create a sense of urgency or encourage offers above a buyer's budget. While these tactics are part of the sales process, they can lead buyers to make decisions driven by fear or emotion rather than clear strategy.

Reviewing contracts is a big part of the property-buying process, but most first-home buyers have never even seen one. Suddenly, you're handed a multi-page document with clauses, legal jargon and timelines and you're expected to know what's risky, normal or what will need extra funds to fix. There's confusion and overwhelm, yet everyone else around you seems to get it.

In chapters 8 and 9, we will offer strategies to help you stay in control, including:

- recognising and responding to common agent tactics
- understanding contract terms before committing
- building negotiation skills and knowing when to walk away.

By approaching interactions with agents and auctioneers from a position of knowledge, buyers can avoid common traps and stay focused on their goals.

6 Using your first property as a foundation

Buying your first property is just phase 1. We'll talk about what comes next and how to make property ownership work for you, your budget and your future goals. It's important to know what happens on the other side: how to handle the mortgage and pay it off sooner; how to protect your assets with wills and estate planning; how to release guarantors; and how to move on to the next property. All of this is covered in chapter 10. Your first property is only the beginning. What comes next is just as important.

A connected web

These six themes are interconnected. A decision in one area often affects others. For example, choosing to buy an investment property first impacts borrowing power, grant eligibility and even the type of mortgage required.

We will take a holistic approach. Instead of treating each issue separately, we will show how the pieces fit together into a complete strategy.

Buying a first property will always involve some level of uncertainty and stress. There will be market fluctuations, competitive auctions and moments of doubt. However, with the right preparation and knowledge, the process can shift from overwhelming to empowering.

The chapters ahead will guide you step by step. You'll learn how to:

- build financial readiness before entering the market
- approach real estate negotiations with confidence
- understand each stage of the buying journey
- plan for all costs, both initial and ongoing
- make decisions that support your long-term goals.

The aim isn't perfection — it's progress. The purpose of this book is to replace confusion with clarity and turn hesitation into action.

The dream of owning your first property is still achievable. With informed choices and a clear strategy, buyers can move forward with confidence and create a secure foundation for their future. Figure 3 probably outlines how you felt over the last little while. If it does resonate with you, you are in the right place.

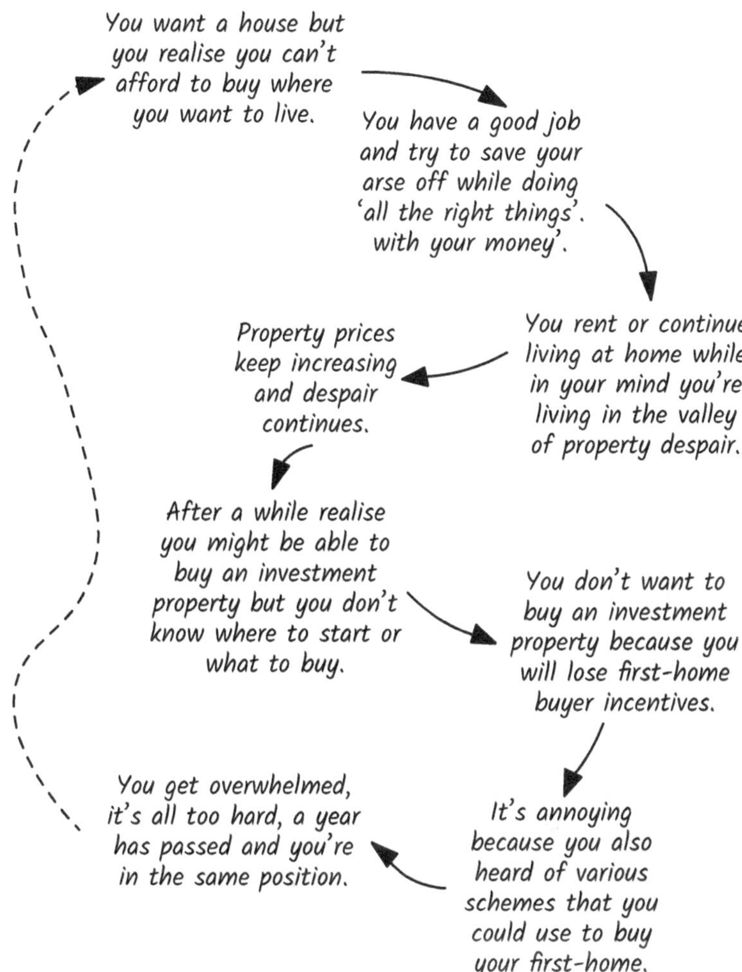

Figure 3: the typical thought process of anyone wanting to buy their first property

One of the biggest unspoken fears for first-home buyers is not the mortgage or the deposit. It's the fear of getting it wrong and being stuck with a mistake they can't undo. This fear is understandable, but it's also overstated. Very few first property

(continued)

purchases are perfect and almost none need to be. Property is not a once-only decision. It's a long-term asset that can usually be rented out, renovated, refinanced or sold if your circumstances change. The idea that your first purchase must be flawless puts unnecessary pressure on a decision that's far more flexible than most people realise.

What matters more than buying the perfect property is buying something that keeps your options open. Properties that appeal to a broad market, sit within your borrowing comfort zone and don't rely on best-case assumptions tend to age well, even if they are not your dream home. Many people who feel like they 'got it wrong' early on still end up in a far stronger position than those who waited years trying to avoid every possible mistake. Progress beats paralysis every time.

Before we begin

There are some common terms you may read in the book or see out in the wild that relate to property, mortgages and finance. But before we get into them, we want to highlight equity.

Equity is one of the most important concepts in property, yet it is often the least understood. Most people rush into buying a home focused on the deposit, the repayments and whether they can 'get approved', without realising that equity is the tool they will be using for decades to come. It influences how you buy, what you buy and what options you will have later. This book makes one thing clear early. Equity is not a buzzword. It is a lever and once you understand it, it changes how you think about property ownership altogether.

At its simplest, equity is the value of a property minus the debt that is owed to anyone (such as a bank, lender or parent). It exists from day one, through your deposit and any grants or concessions, and it grows over time as the property value increases and your loan reduces.

Your first property is always the hardest because you must create that equity yourself through saving. Every property after that becomes easier, not because you earn more or work harder, but because equity has been quietly building in the background without you lifting a finger.

Throughout this book, we unpack equity in plain English and show how it can be used deliberately rather than accidentally. Whether it's upgrading your home, buying an investment property, renovating or even investing outside property altogether, equity is the common thread. Buy the wrong asset and the lack of equity can trap you, as can the wrong structure. Buy the right one and it becomes one of the most powerful tools you'll ever use. That's why understanding equity comes before everything else.

Okay, now we're going to highlight some of the baseline investing terminology and acronyms that you need to know if you're new to property.

Body corporate / strata fees

Regular payments owners make for shared spaces like gardens, lifts, building insurance, maintenance and driveways in apartments or townhouses.

Building inspection / pest inspection

A professional check of the property before buying. Looks for structural issues, termites and other hidden problems. Highly recommended.

Buyer's agent / advocate

A property professional engaged and paid for by the buyer to find, assess and negotiate the purchase of a property. The terms are used interchangeably depending on where you live, not just state based. This can be capital city or regional dialect! A buyers agent works for you, not the owner of the property or 'vendor'.

Capital growth

When a property's value increases over time. This is often where long-term wealth is built.

Comparison rate

Shows the true cost of a loan once most fees and charges are included. In Australia, lenders must display a comparison rate alongside any advertised interest rate so borrowers can compare loans fairly.

By law, examples are usually based on a $150 000 loan over 30 years under the National Credit Code. The comparison rate factors in interest plus common fees such as establishment and monthly charges.

Conveyancing

The legal process of transferring property ownership from the seller to the buyer. This is handled by a conveyancer or solicitor.

Cost base

The starting value used to calculate capital gains tax (CGT). It includes the purchase price plus costs like stamp duty, legal fees and other buying expenses. For example, if you buy for $700 000 and pay $25 000 in stamp duty your cost base is $725 000.

Deposit

Money paid upfront when buying a property. Usually a percentage of the purchase price, often 10 per cent. Some buying structures reduce the cash deposit, but a deposit is still part of the contract.

Deposit bond

A guarantee used instead of paying a cash deposit. It covers the deposit amount and usually requires vendor approval. Common when funds are tied up elsewhere. Basically you pay a fee to a company to cover your lack of deposit but you are still liable to pay it if you pull out of the contract.

Exchange

When buyer and seller sign and swap contracts. The sale becomes legally binding and a deposit is usually paid. Settlement happens later.

First Home Owner Grant (FHOG)

A government payment to help eligible first-home buyers. Amounts and eligibility vary by state. Many schemes are loosely called FHOG, which can be misleading.

Fixed rate

Not impacted by economic or market conditions, or lender decisions, for the period of the loan.

Gross vs net rental yield

Gross yield is rent before expenses. Net yield is after costs like council rates, insurance, maintenance and property management.

Home loan features / flexibility

Loan features such as offset accounts, redraw facilities, extra repayments, loan portability and split loans.

Interest

The cost charged by a lender for borrowing money.

Interest-only loan

You pay only the interest for a set period. Repayments are lower initially, but the loan balance does not reduce during this time.

Land tax

A state-based tax charged on investment properties, generally not on your primary residence.

Lenders Mortgage Insurance (LMI)

If your deposit is under 20 per cent, lenders usually require LMI to protect themselves if you default. It is a once-off premium and can often be added to the loan. *Important:* LMI protects the lender, not you.

Loan-to-Value Ratio (LVR)

The loan amount compared to the property's value, expressed as a percentage. For example, a $355 000 loan on an $800 000 property equals a 44.4 per cent LVR, which means you have 55.6 per cent equity in the property. A lower LVR is generally better. If your LVR was 0, you would have no debt.

LVR bands

Different interest rates offered by lenders depending on your LVR, such as under or over 80 per cent.

Mortgage broker

A professional who compares loans from multiple lenders and helps you apply for the right one. Brokers act as the middle person and are usually paid by the lender, not you, although they work for you.

Negative gearing

When expenses for an investment property are higher than your income on the property, you are running negative (or at a loss). The loss may be claimed against taxable income.

Offset account

A bank account linked to your loan. The balance offsets the loan amount and reduces interest charged.

For example, if you had a mortgage of $600 000 and had a linked offset account with $50 000 in it, you would only be charged interest on $550 000. The account with $50 000 in it would not earn interest.

Positive cash flow / positive gearing

When rental income covers all costs and still leaves surplus cash.

Pre-approval

A conditional approval from a lender showing how much you can borrow before you start house hunting.

Principal

The original loan amount you owe, excluding interest.

Property Exchange Australia (PEXA)

The national digital platform used to settle property transactions electronically. Your conveyancer manages this and passes on a small fee.

Redraw facility

Allows you to access extra repayments you have made on top of required repayments. Scheduled repayments cannot be redrawn.

Refinancing

Replacing your existing loan with a new one to secure a better rate or improved features or structure.

Rental yield (yield)

Annual rent expressed as a percentage of the property's value. Usually quoted as gross yield; however, you may see net yield mentioned, which is after property expenses (such as agent fees, insurance etc.)

For example, $505 per week on a $750 000 property equals a 3.5 per cent yield. (($505 × 52) ÷ $750 000 = 3.5%)

Repricing

Negotiating a lower interest rate with your existing lender without changing loans. Often handled by a mortgage broker.

Scenario

Different loan or buying options modelled by a broker to show how repayments, borrowing power and flexibility change under different structures.

Settlement

The day ownership officially transfers and money changes hands.

Stamp duty

A state government tax paid when purchasing property. Rates vary by state, generally a percentage of the sale price. This is a once-off cost.

Variable rate

An interest rate that can move up or down in response to economic and market conditions, as well as lender decisions. Repayments can change over the period of the loan.

Vendor / seller

The person or entity selling the property.

Withdrawal / cooling-off period

A short period after signing a contract where the buyer can withdraw, subject to state rules and penalties.

Zoning / land use

Planning rules that define how land can be used, such as residential, commercial or development potential.

This is *The Quick-Start Guide to Your First Property.*

Know your 'why'

The property-buying process has many similarities to leadership. Not leadership in the corporate sense, but personal leadership: the ability to make clear decisions, stay focused when things get uncomfortable and follow through over time.

The four Ds

Across many leadership frameworks, one commonly referenced model is the four Ds: Desire, Determination, Dedication and Discipline. When you overlay these four traits with the journey of buying your first property, the parallels become obvious. Buying property is not passive. It requires you to lead yourself well.

Desire

Desire is your 'why'. It's the emotional driver behind wanting to buy property in the first place. This could be stability, freedom, a sense of progress or creating options for your future. The desire may feel obvious, but it's worth pressure-testing it. Many of the exercises around finding your why are designed to help you connect emotionally, not just intellectually, to the goal. Be careful though. Some prompts may reveal that the desire is not strong enough right now, or that it's more of a 'someday' goal than a short- or medium-term one. That insight is not a failure. It's clarity.

Determination

Determination is what carries you through friction. This is where the process gets real. Paperwork, saving constraints, lending rules, delayed timelines and moments of doubt all show up here. Determination is not about being stubborn. It's about staying engaged when progress feels slow and adjusting your approach without abandoning the goal. Most people who stall in their property journey do not lack information, they lose determination when the process takes longer or feels harder than expected.

Dedication

Dedication is the willingness to prioritise the goal consistently over time. This might mean saying no to certain lifestyle upgrades, sticking to a savings plan or regularly checking in on your progress instead of avoiding it. This is where buying property moves from intention to behaviour. Dedication is shown in small, repeated actions. Reviewing your numbers, keeping documents up to date and staying in contact with the right professionals even when there's no immediate reward.

Discipline

Discipline is doing the boring but necessary things, even when motivation dips. This includes budgeting, managing spending, maintaining communication with your partner and not drifting off plan when something shiny appears. Discipline creates momentum. It's what turns desire into outcomes. Without discipline, the goal remains theoretical. With it, buying your first property becomes a sequence of manageable steps rather than an overwhelming leap.

You don't need to become a 'leader' to buy property. But you do need to lead yourself. When you approach the property buying-process through the lens of the four Ds, you give yourself a framework for staying grounded, focused and realistic from start to finish.

One of the biggest challenges when buying a property is staying engaged either with your savings plan, or property search, for the long haul. This is going to take time and if you have a spouse or partner who isn't as on board as you, it's only going to make the whole process harder. Anyone who has achieved anything great has coupled sacrifice and time together. In the quest for your first property you need to know that six months is considered a short amount of time so start to get match fit and get used to incorporating the 4Ds into your lifestyle. Think of this period of time as bootcamp for property. The good news is that what you put attention to will yield results, so imagine what would happen if you applied laser-focused attention to your property quest for the long term.

You'll be tempted along the way. That's not a maybe; that's a certainty.

'Want to come and see Sabrina Carpenter when she comes to Australia?'

No, I'm saving for my first property.

'You need a new air conditioner in your car and it will be $1500 to fix, so you should just buy a new car!'

No. Spending $1500 is less than $15 000, or more with a car loan. I'm saving for my first property.

'Rentvesting sounds complicated. Why don't you just wait another year and see what happens?'

No, waiting without a plan is just procrastination with better PR. I'm moving forward now. (We'll talk about rentvesting in chapter 6.)

'Interest rates are high. Maybe property isn't a good idea anymore.'

No, cycles change. Preparation and discipline matter more than perfect timing and I'm playing the long game.

You really must bake into your mindset that your first property purchase may take some time, require sacrifices and you'll need the four Ds to rinse and repeat.

Buying your first property is hard enough on your own. Doing it with a partner who is not aligned makes it significantly harder. This doesn't mean you need identical money personalities, but you do need agreement on the destination and the trade-offs required to get there. If one of you is in 'property bootcamp' mode while the other is still spending like nothing has changed, friction is guaranteed.

Before you get deep into saving or inspecting properties, have an honest conversation about what the next six to 24 months will actually look like. What are you both saying no to? What are you prioritising? What sacrifices are temporary and what's non-negotiable?

This is where the four Ds need to show up as a team sport. Shared desire keeps you emotionally connected to the goal. Determination helps you push through the boring and uncomfortable parts together. Dedication shows up in daily decisions that reflect the plan, not impulse. Discipline is sticking to the agreement even when temptation knocks loudly.

When partners are aligned, progress feels lighter. When they are not, every financial decision becomes a negotiation. Property rewards patience, consistency and teamwork. Get on the same page early and the rest of the process becomes far more manageable. Use this process as a flashpoint for the relationship and do not be afraid to get some couples counselling to really ensure you are both aligned with this property venture—and also other areas!

Your behaviour is driven by your 'why'. Truly ask yourself, 'Why do I want to get into property?' As beautifully complex humans we often have greater needs or desires driving us and our decisions without realising it and it's crucial to understand what's happening behind the scenes. This helps us line up the right path to owning a property. Read the statements below and see which ones resonate with you.

'I just really *want a home of my own.'*

If this is you, we hear how important this is and completely respect how emotional the idea of owning your own home (*your* own home) can be. A home becomes a key part of your identity and memories—it's where you celebrate birthdays, invite friends around and build families. There really is no greater feeling than knowing that where you sleep every night is yours and you can adjust the space to suit your lifestyle and wishes. With this book, together we can find your way there.

'I'm done with renting! I hate the instability, I hate moving, I want security and to be able to change things in my home the way I want.'

If you're tired of a lack of stability—tired of rental inspections, rent hikes and packing boxes every year—buying your own home can bring a real sense of stability and control. There's comfort in knowing that no-one can suddenly sell the property from under you or stop you hanging a picture on the wall. It's about more than owning an asset; it's about putting down roots and feeling secure in your space.

The step from renting to owning is a big one and it's worth going in with a clear plan. Start with your borrowing capacity and budget: not just what the bank says, what you're comfortable to afford. Think about location, lifestyle, compromises you're willing to make to enter the market sooner. The goal is not perfection — it's stability and the long-term benefit of being a home owner.

'I'm not sure I'm going to be able to afford to buy where I want to live. What options are there for me to get into the market?'

This is where a lot more first-home buyers are finding themselves with the current state of property markets around the country. Rentvesters are born here — in this thought process — rather than deciding to become a rentvester out of a financial strategy. Not being able to afford to buy where you want to live and not wanting to move should not rule you out of the property market. It's about pivoting, looking at all your options and making a decision that's right for you. To make an informed decision, you first need to know all of the options that are open to you.

'I don't ever plan on buying a home to live in, but I do want to grow wealth through property.'

You are an investor — a property investor. Your focus will be finding the right asset, a property that performs well and allows further growth of your portfolio. The right type of asset and location for your first purchase will be important, as will your finance structure to ensure you are setting yourself up for the longer term plan.

The key to this strategy is removing emotion and thinking about numbers first. You'll want to assess cash flow, understand the costs of holding a property and choose locations with strong fundamentals like infrastructure growth, employment hubs and limited housing supply. Interest-only loans and offset accounts will be key in your finance strategy as your goal is to hold more property, and available cash can make a huge difference to your options.

Remember you aren't buying a home but a vehicle for wealth creation. Treat it like a business decision, not a lifestyle one, and your first investment can be your launchpad for financial freedom.

'My goal is to get into the market asap — where I live is secondary to this.'

If your goal is to get into the market as soon as possible, you're already thinking like an investor, even if you don't think of yourself as one yet. The mindset is all about momentum, building equity, learning the process and positioning yourself for your next move. Where you live is secondary; your first property is a steppingstone not a destination. Your focus will be on buying property in growth areas, adding value through improvements and using this property as a springboard for your next move.

'I'm not ready to settle down. I may work elsewhere to where I buy but want to consider getting into the market early.'

A common strategy is to buy property to live in for now not knowing your plan. It's okay to buy without knowing your big plan. A lot of people wait until they know the big plan but we'll let you in on a secret: a lot of people never know their big plan. They take action with the tools they have at the time and when they look back realise they never actually had it figured out.

If your work isn't stable, property might not be the best fit right now. But if you're moving around or planning big life changes and you're still happy to take on the responsibility, don't rule it out just because things feel uncertain.

'I want to save up and buy where I am. I love where I live and plan to stay here.'

This one is about the emotional pull of a particular place. Where you live shapes your lifestyle, your friendships, your routines and your work opportunities. This is the most common driving force for first-home buyers. They are buying a home to live in and already live in the area they would like to be in the long term. They may move one day but it's not on the cards right now and they may like to upsize down the track but they are pretty settled in their area. They have family or friends in the area and their work is here. They have a community they wish to stay close with. If this is your plan, the focus is about looking at what you can buy in the area you wish to be a part of and making a decision based on this along with what you can afford.

A few questions to consider:

- How much are you willing to trade off for location?
- Would a smaller home or unit in your preferred area make you happier than a larger house elsewhere?
- Would buying in the area you want to live put you at risk financially? Would you be overcommitting mortgage wise?
- If you have a dream suburb and that is key for you yet a house is not affordable, maybe rethinking the kind of property you buy is necessary. And always remember, your first home is just that: your first home. The majority of people don't end up where they first buy but their first home was integral for the next steps.

Why getting in early matters

Getting into the property market early has been the secret weapon for a lot of people who've built solid financial security. But let's be honest: for many young Aussies today, buying a place feels about as achievable as winning a renovation reality TV show. The old 'save a deposit, buy a house down the road' formula just isn't the go anymore. To make it happen, you'll need to think differently from how your parents did, and that's totally okay. In fact, we'd go as far as to say it's the only approach that really works now.

We've never had someone come to us a decade after buying a home and say, 'Honestly, we should've waited'. But we have heard plenty of regrets from people who could have bought earlier and didn't. Our goal is to give you the best shot at getting into the market as early as makes sense for your life, not with pressure, but with clarity and confidence. When you're ready to buy, we want you to understand the process, make informed decisions and have the right people around you so the whole experience feels less stressful.

One of the big reasons property has helped so many Aussies build wealth is simple: over the long term, values tend to rise. Our market is pretty unique in that way. Steady growth has made property a go-to asset for both homeowners and investors. But if you're living in or around a capital city, you've probably looked at prices online and thought: 'How on earth will I ever buy here?' Or you've imagined finally scraping in…only to be chained to a monster mortgage. Totally normal thoughts and exactly why thinking creatively about how and where you buy can make the whole thing feel far less overwhelming. There are more options than you might realise and exploring them can open doors you didn't know existed.

> Why your 'why' matters more than anything else:
>
> * It drives better decisions.
> * It helps you understand your own priorities before starting the process.
> * It helps you focus on the strategies that will actually work for you.

Turn off comparison

Personal finance is exactly that: personal. Everyone has different incomes, expenses, lifestyles and goals, which means there's no point comparing your journey to someone else's.

Sure, you might scroll past a friend online who's earning more and getting into property faster, and that's great for them! But it doesn't make your own path any less valid. Especially for younger generations, the road into property looks very different today than it has for decades.

The key is to focus on what you can achieve right now. Buy the best asset you can with the resources and lending options available to you. That — not someone else's timeline — is what gets you closer to your dreams.

Don't wait for a magic solution

Now is not the time to sit and wait for an inheritance, or for markets to 'crash' before you purchase your first property. The best thing you can do is understand your 'why' and build a plan that makes that 'why' happen. Once you know the reason you want to buy — security, freedom, stability or a stepping stone to build wealth—you can stop outsourcing your future to luck, timing or someone else's plan. Taking action, even small steps, puts you back in the driver's seat.

> A common concern is what happens if life doesn't follow the plan. Relationships end. Jobs change. Kids arrive earlier or later than expected. Health issues pop up. This isn't failure, it's life. Your first property doesn't need to perfectly match your future self. It just needs to be resilient enough to adapt as your life evolves. That might mean a property that can be rented out if you need to move, or one that doesn't stretch your cash flow so tightly that one change knocks everything over.
>
> Many people worry that buying a home locks them in forever. In reality, most first properties become stepping stones rather than destinations. Homes turn into investments. Investments turn into deposits for the next place. Sometimes people sell and reset. None of these outcomes mean you failed. Planning for flexibility from the start is one of the smartest things you can do and it allows you to move forward without needing your entire future mapped out in advance.

Turning your 'why' into a property brief

Knowing why you want to buy property isn't a fluffy exercise. It's a practical filter that shapes what you buy, where you buy, how much risk you take and how you behave when emotions run high.

Your 'why' turns an abstract goal into a property brief. Without it, buyers tend to drift, react or copy what others are doing. With it, decisions become clearer, trade-offs become easier and confidence improves even when the market feels noisy.

When we asked our podcast listeners about property and their 'why', two dominant motivations consistently appeared. Security and stability on one hand and wealth creation on the other. Many buyers sit somewhere in the middle, and that's completely normal. The key is knowing which one is driving your decisions right now.

Why I want security and a place of my own

For many first-home buyers, security is the primary driver. This often shows up as wanting stability, control and relief from the uncertainty of renting. Concerns about rising rents, lease terminations, moving costs and feeling like you're always living in someone else's space came through strongly in our survey.

If security is your core motivation, your property brief will likely prioritise liveability over optimisation. This doesn't mean ignoring long-term value, but it does mean choosing a property you're genuinely comfortable living in.

This usually looks like:

- buying in a location that supports your lifestyle, work and personal networks
- choosing a property you could see yourself living in for several years
- prioritising functionality, layout and comfort over speculative upside.

For some buyers, this may require a difficult but honest conversation about location. If you can't afford to buy where you currently live, you may need to consider adjusting expectations, compromising on property type or exploring relocation. Security comes from ownership that's sustainable, not ownership at any cost.

A security-led 'why' also helps protect you from emotional overspending. When the focus is on stability, buyers are often more disciplined about not stretching themselves to the limit just to secure something marginally better.

Why I want to build wealth early

Another common motivation is using property as a tool to build wealth. Buyers driven by this 'why' tend to be more comfortable separating where they live from where they invest, especially early on.

This group often values:

- capital growth potential over short-term comfort
- buying earlier rather than waiting for perfection
- being open to rentvesting or buying where they can afford rather than where they ideally want to live.

A wealth-focused property brief usually includes consideration of growth corridors, infrastructure plans, employment hubs and long-term demand drivers. These buyers are often more analytical and less emotionally attached to the property itself.

However, this approach requires clarity. Without a strong 'why', buyers aiming for wealth can get stuck in analysis paralysis or constantly second-guess whether they are making the optimal decision.

Your 'why' keeps the strategy grounded. It reminds you that the goal is progress, not perfection.

When you don't know your why

When we surveyed our listeners, a clear pattern emerged. Those who had already purchased a property consistently pointed to the same mistakes, most of which stemmed from being unclear on their underlying motivation.

Here are some to consider:

- *Overstretching*
  When emotions take over, buyers can spend more than they intended because the property 'feels right' in the moment. Without a clear why, it becomes easy to justify decisions that undermine long-term financial comfort.

- *Underbuying*
  On the other end of the spectrum, some buyers play it so safe that they purchase a property that doesn't meet their needs or support their goals. This can lead to early regret, forced upgrades or unnecessary transaction costs.

- *FOMO-driven decisions*
  In hot markets, fear-of-missing-out can override logic. Buyers rush decisions, skip due diligence or compromise on fundamentals. A strong 'why' acts as an anchor when the market feels frantic.

- *Too many outside voices*
  Friends, family, social media and headlines all have opinions. Without clarity, buyers can become paralysed or pulled in conflicting directions. Your 'why' helps you filter advice rather than absorb it all.

> Family advice can be one of the most confusing parts of buying a first property. Parents and relatives often mean well, but their experience is usually based on a very different market, different lending rules and very different price points. What worked for them may no longer be realistic or even relevant. This can leave buyers torn between professional advice and family expectations, especially when emotions and money mix.
>
> The challenge is learning how to listen without outsourcing your decisions. Useful advice tends to be specific, informed and aligned with your goals. Unhelpful advice often sounds absolute, fear-based or nostalgic. You are allowed to thank people for their input and still choose a different path. Your first property needs to work for your life, not someone else's memory of the market 20 or 30 years ago.

A clear 'why' doesn't guarantee perfect decisions, but it dramatically reduces regret.

Your why will change, and that's okay

Your motivation for buying property isn't fixed. In fact, it's expected to evolve as your life changes. You may start with a desire for independence or financial momentum. Later, priorities might shift to family, schooling, community or long-term lifestyle. The important thing is not consistency over decades, but clarity at each stage.

The response to our survey showed many buyers felt pressure to 'get it right forever' with their first purchase. This mindset often leads to delays or unrealistic expectations. Your first property doesn't need to solve every future problem. It needs to align with your current why and your current capacity. As long as your why is clear at the time of purchase, your strategy can evolve with you.

Your why and your professional team

When you start working with professionals such as brokers, buyers' agents, accountants and conveyancers, your why becomes incredibly useful. It gives context to your numbers and direction to your strategy.

Professionals can help you with the how, but only if the why is clear. When you articulate your motivation, your team can:

- structure lending to support your priorities
- suggest property types and locations that fit your goals
- help you understand trade-offs rather than default options.

Without this clarity, advice can become generic or misaligned.

Property in action

Rather than treating your why as a one-off exercise, turn it into a simple reference point you can revisit.

Consider the following prompts and reflect on them as a complete statement rather than isolated answers:

- Why you want to buy property right now?
- What do you want this purchase to do for your life over the next phase?
- How this property supports that outcome.

For example, your internal statement might read like one of the following:

- 'I want to buy property to start building long-term wealth early. My goal is to get into the market in a sustainable way and let time do the heavy lifting. This property supports that by being in an area with long-term growth drivers, even if it's not where I live right now.'
- 'I want to buy property because time in the market matters more to me than buying my forever home straight away. My goal is to get started with a property that can grow in value and create options later. This property supports that by being in a location with strong long-term demand, solid fundamentals and a price point I can comfortably hold.'
- 'I want to buy property because stability matters more now that my life has more moving parts. My goal is to live somewhere that supports family routines, schooling and a sense of community over the long term. This property supports that by being practical, affordable to hold and in an area we can realistically stay in for years.'

Keep your statement in mind throughout the process. When decisions feel difficult, return to it. If a choice doesn't align with your why, it deserves closer scrutiny.

Our lived examples

Rach's experience reflects how a property plan can evolve alongside your why.

In her 20s, the goal was simple. Build financial independence. Lifestyle took a back seat as she rented modestly while purchasing where it made sense financially. The focus was on properties that aligned with a long-term wealth goal, not emotional attachment.

In her 30s and as a parent, the why shifted. Schooling, community, neighbours and emotional security became priorities. The property strategy changed accordingly. The earlier decisions created options and the later decisions prioritised lifestyle.

Neither phase was right or wrong. Each was aligned with a clear why at the time.

For Glen, his initial why for his first home was about 50/50. His first home was purchased when he was 31 years old. He knew that he didn't enjoy renting and was building a business at the time, so stability was his goal. He is also a more conservative personality and the thought of always having to move caused some anxiety. At the same time, he knew that the right purchase could have a longer term financial upside. This, coupled with him being a spender-type personality, meant having a mortgage and some financial pressure in that area of his life (paying down a home loan) would provide some forced savings!

At the time, he had a state-based stamp duty exemption, a cash grant for a brand-new home (he was lucky enough to buy a brand-new townhouse) and he knew it was going to be a stepping stone so he set his mortgage up with a view that it would be an investment property one day. Glen now rents and has investment properties and as he is established in his career and business, needing to move around isn't as stressful.

The point is nothing is forever and your why for your first property purchase will change in the years after your purchase—and that's okay.

Start with this...

There's plenty to consider for your own situation. Have a think about:

* Which of the 4Ds you struggle with. How can you lead yourself better?
* Your 'why'. Why are you buying a property? What's driving you?

Setting up your foundations

By this point, you should be clear on why you want to buy a property.

You might be working towards a home to live in, a stepping stone into the market or your first investment property. Whatever your strategy, you are no longer browsing property as a vague idea. You are preparing to make a decision that will shape your finances and lifestyle for years to come.

This chapter is where intention turns into structure.

Before we talk about suburbs, deposits, lending policies or open homes, we need to make sure the foundations of your financial life are strong enough to support property ownership. Not just buying a property, but holding it through interest rate changes, life changes and unexpected events.

To explain this, we are going to use a framework we rely on heavily in our work: 'Glen James' sound financial house' (see figure 2.1).

Yes, we are aware of the irony of using a house diagram in a property book. But it fits! Property is not just a purchase. It is something you live in, service, maintain and plan around. And like any house, if the foundations are weak, cracks appear when pressure is applied.

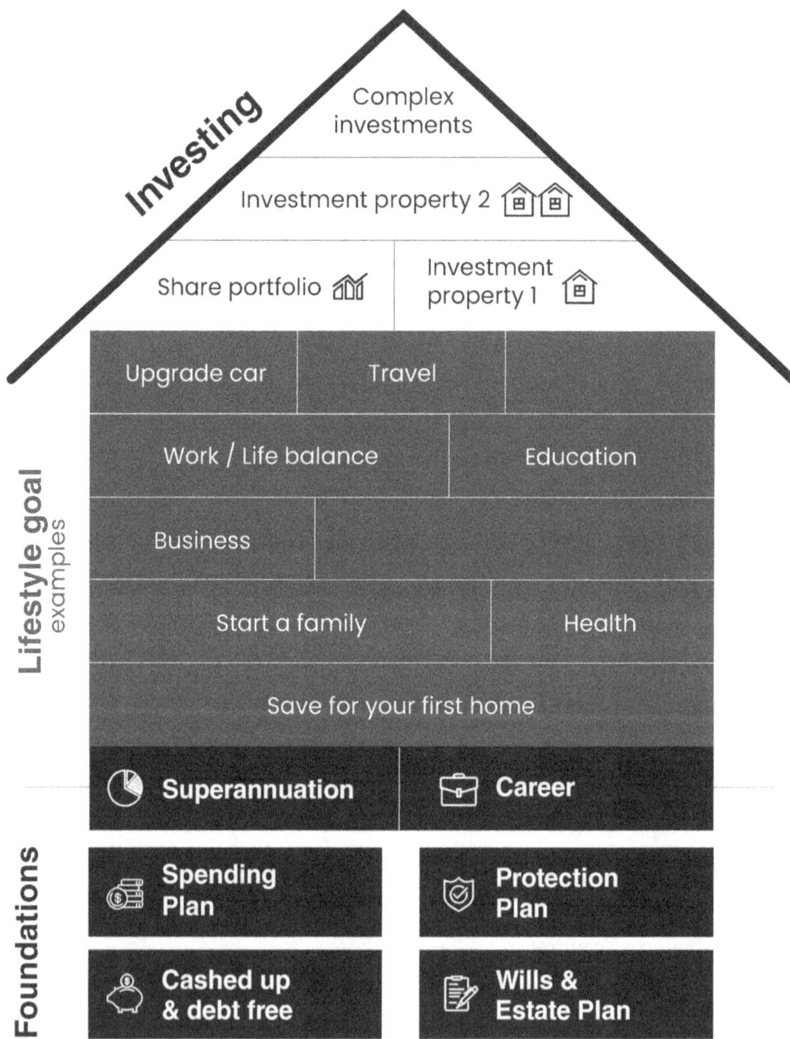

Figure 2.1: Glen's sound financial house structure

Why foundations matter more than speed

If you were building a real house, you wouldn't start with the roof. You wouldn't start with the walls. You wouldn't even start with the slab. You would start with the foundations.

In construction, foundations must be inspected and approved before anything else can be built. If they are not reinforced properly, everything that sits on top of them is at risk, no matter how good it looks on the surface. Your finances work the same way.

We have seen many people rush into property because they were worried about missing out, falling behind or doing what everyone else seemed to be doing, and then find themselves in mortgage stress or needing to sell with a life change. The problem was never property itself. The problem was that the foundations underneath it weren't ready. There's also an argument that the bedrock that your foundations sit on is your 'why' and your mindset!

The point of the sound financial house is to slow things down just enough to get the order right.

The sound financial house explained

At the base of the sound financial house are four foundations. These are the non-negotiables. They are the things you should work towards having in place before you seriously commit to buying your first home or first investment property.

Those foundations are:

1. a spending plan
2. being cashed up and free of consumer debt
3. a protection plan
4. wills and estate planning.

These foundations support everything else in your financial life. On top of the foundations sits the slab of the house. This is made up of your career and superannuation. These are your long-term income engines. They quietly do the heavy lifting in the background while you work towards your goals. The walls of the house represent your lifestyle goals. This is where saving for your first home or first investment property usually sits, alongside goals such as travel, health, education, starting a family or building a business. The roof represents investing: share portfolios, investment properties and eventually more complex strategies. The order matters. When people experience financial stress, it's rarely because they moved too slowly. It's usually because they skipped steps, much like anything in life.

Foundation 1: A spending plan

Everything in your financial life starts with cash flow. Money comes in. Money goes out. If you don't have a clear system for tracking this, you're guessing. Guessing might work for a short period of time. It doesn't work when you're trying to save a deposit, qualify for a loan or manage a mortgage over the years.

A spending plan isn't about cutting every joy out of your life. It's about understanding where your money actually goes so you can make deliberate decisions. Even if you were able to buy a property tomorrow through a parental guarantee or government scheme, poor money habits would follow you into ownership. Rates, insurance, strata fees, maintenance and repairs don't care how you got into the property. You'd likely end up with more consumer debt and chaos. We want your property purchase to be a blessing, not a curse. Without a spending plan, people often feel like they earn good money but never seem to get ahead. With a spending plan, progress becomes visible and repeatable.

Foundation 2: Cashed up and debt free

Property ownership rewards resilience. Things go wrong. Cars break down. Hot water systems fail. Medical bills appear. Jobs change. Life happens. Being cashed up means having an emergency fund. A realistic target is around three months of core living expenses. This isn't an investment account. It's a buffer. Its job is to stop emergencies turning into debt. Being debt free means eliminating consumer debt. Credit cards you can't clear each month. Personal loans. Buy-now-pay-later balances. These are usually a sign that spending has outpaced income.

From a lender's perspective, consumer debt reduces your borrowing capacity. From your perspective, it reduces flexibility and increases stress. For every $10 000 of consumer debt you have, your borrowing capacity could reduce by up to and over $30 000 to $50 000 (depending on the lender). That $30 000 car loan could be stopping you from borrowing the extra $150 000 that you need to get into the property.

When people buy property without a buffer, every unexpected cost feels like a crisis. When they buy with one, problems are annoying but manageable. Cash buys options. Debt removes them.

Foundation 3: A protection plan

Every financial plan relies on income. Banks lend to income, not potential. If you're unable to work due to illness or injury, income protection insurance is what keeps money flowing into your spending plan. Without it, emergency funds drain quickly. This becomes even more important once you own property. If your income stops and you can't make your repayments, the bank doesn't absorb the loss. Eventually, the property is at risk. Financial stress on top of medical stress or stress from an accident. No thanks. If you have dependents, or soon will, life insurance also becomes part of this foundation. The goal is not to insure every scenario. The goal is to ensure your plan still works if something outside your control happens. If you have a family, please get death cover, as a minimum. Insurance isn't pessimism. It's acknowledging reality and preparing for it.

The good news is that if you speak with a financial adviser (don't go to your superfund, the cover is generally not as good nor as cost-effective as going through a financial adviser), they can advise you on the appropriate levels of cover required based on your situation. The premiums can be funded from your super, and the cost of the income protection insurance is generally tax deductible. Please factor this into your spending plan.

Foundation 4: Wills and estate planning

This is often overlooked, especially by first-time buyers. But it matters far more once property enters the picture. If you die owning property in your own name, the executor of your estate will usually need to go through a legal process called probate before the property can be sold or transferred. This is how the courts confirm that the will is valid and that the executor has authority to act.

Without a will, the process is slower and more complex. The court appoints an administrator and your estate is distributed according to state intestacy laws. These rules may not reflect your wishes at all. If property is involved, delays can create real problems. Mortgages still need to be serviced. Rates and insurance still apply. Families are left managing legal processes while dealing with grief. A will simplifies this. It's not just a legal document—it's a practical one. It reduces stress for the people you leave behind and ensures your assets flow where you intend them to go.

Estate planning also includes documents such as a power of attorney. These allow someone you trust to act on your behalf if you are unable to make decisions due to illness or incapacity. This document stops being relevant when you die, but it's critical while you're alive. If you own property, or are planning to, estate planning isn't optional housekeeping—it's part of responsible ownership. This can be sorted while you're saving and planning your purchase.

The slab of the house: Career and superannuation

Once the foundations are in place, we look at the slab of the house. Your career is one of the biggest drivers of your property journey. Income determines how much you can borrow, how quickly you can save and how resilient you are when circumstances change. For some people, this means asking hard questions. If income is limited, property may need to be a medium-term goal while career progression takes priority. This isn't failure. It's sequencing, and that's okay. For others, income may be stable but capped. Teachers, nurses and public-sector workers often fall into this category. In these cases, the conversation isn't about changing careers, but about exploring ways to increase income within that career over time. You need to focus on job opportunities within your current industry and training, not so much a career overhaul. Like your industry but need more money? Can you do something else within your industry?

Superannuation also sits here. If you have a job, you have super. It compounds quietly in the background while you focus on nearer term goals like buying property. It isn't something to ignore, but it's also not something to over-complicate at this stage. The slab doesn't need to be perfect. It needs to be solid enough to support what comes next.

Building in the right order

The walls of the sound financial house represent your lifestyle goals. For pretty much all readers of this book, saving for a first home or first investment property is the primary one.

The roof comes last. Investing in shares, additional properties or more complex strategies works best once the foundations are solid and the walls are stable. Trying to invest before the foundations are in place often leads to forced sales, poor timing and unnecessary stress. It's easy to get invested. It's much harder to stay invested. You don't need everything sorted before you begin saving for property. But you do need a framework that keeps decisions aligned and progress sustainable.

This chapter is about structure and order. In the chapters that follow, we'll get practical. We'll talk about money systems, borrowing, strategies and decision making. But first, we build the foundations.

Property in action

Based on the sound financial house we've just discussed, what is missing in your own life? Take one step today to sort that one piece that's missing.

Your career matters more than you think

Although we only touch on it in the sound financial house, your career is your best investment because it compounds harder than almost anything else you will ever put money into. Skills stack. Experience stacks. Reputation stacks. A single course, qualification, promotion or sideways move into a higher value role can lift your income for decades. That extra income then funds everything else. Your savings rate improves. Your super grows faster. Your investing options widen. Shares and property love cash flow and your career is the machine that produces it. Ignore your career and you're trying to build wealth with one hand tied behind your back.

> From a pure money sense, returns on career investment are often obscene. A few thousand dollars spent on education or a strategic career pivot can turn into hundreds of thousands over a working life. Try getting that risk-adjusted return anywhere else without sweating (this is a fancy way of saying you don't need to put $100 000 into an investment hoping it doubles as it would be considered extremely high risk). People obsess over picking the perfect high interest bank account, ETF, superannuation fund or property, but underinvest in the thing that determines how much they can actually invest. That's backwards. Your career is the income engine. Investments are just the storage unit.

There's also the life satisfaction angle, which matters more than most people admit. You spend a frightening amount of your waking hours working. If your career is misaligned with your values, strengths or interests, it bleeds into everything. Stress follows you home. Motivation disappears. Burnout creeps in quietly and then crashes the party. A career that fits reasonably well doesn't need to be perfect or Instagram worthy. It just needs to be sustainable, stimulating enough and aligned with the life you want to live. That's a massive quality-of-life upgrade.

The best part is that career investment gives you optionality. More skills and credibility means more choices. You can negotiate better, say 'no' more often, take time off without panic or pivot when life changes. That freedom is the real dividend. Money helps, but control over your time and energy is the endgame. Invest in your career early and consistently and it quietly props up every other part of your financial life. Ignore it and no spreadsheet in the world will save you.

This isn't to say if you want more money just get a higher paying job. This is to say you spend a lot of time working and you should enjoy it. You should also want to ensure you have the maximum trade-off between the time that is traded for money from your job. There can be extra benefits too, depending on your career, when it comes to obtaining a mortgage (such as lower deposits for certain professionals) although these are considered secondary to setting up your life and career, which gives you satisfaction on top of money.

So, what would you rather have? A property now that's attainable but not really meeting any goal or metric, where you're stuck in your job and generally hate life? Or do you want to wait a year or so and sort out your career, so you don't hate life, and then get your property (while saving along the way)? This isn't black or white—life is grey and thought exercises rarely translate to reality—but it's good to consider.

The four budget levers

When managing your money, budget or spending plan, Glen teaches that there are *only four budget levers you can pull* to speed up your deposit savings. That's it. No secret hack. Everyone who gets there faster simply pulls these levers harder, for longer or more deliberately than others. The aim is to widen the gap between income and expenses, then defend that gap until the deposit is done.

Increase income

This is the most powerful lever, and it doesn't need to be complicated. Increasing income might come from a pay rise, promotion, changing employers, overtime or additional work for a defined season. This is different from the big career discussion as it could be a short-term lever pull. Even relatively small increases can materially shorten your deposit timeline when they're consistently saved. This lever works best when income increases are intentional and tied directly to the goal, rather than absorbed into lifestyle creep.

Decrease savings

This is technically a budget lever, but when you're saving for a property deposit, it's the one lever we do *not* want you pulling. Saving less moves you backwards and undermines the habit you're trying to build. In genuine emergencies, this lever may be used temporarily, but in deposit mode, savings are non-negotiable. If things feel tight, the answer is almost never to save less. The answer is to earn more or spend better. The reason this lever is here is you may wish to keep your financial lifestyle and don't really have the time or capacity to increase your income.

Review a line item

Reviewing means keeping the category but optimising the cost. You're not cutting everything. You're making smarter choices. Downgrading a gym membership, switching providers, reducing how often you eat out, renegotiating bills or trimming subscriptions. This lever is powerful because it finds money without making life miserable. You're still living. You're just living with intention. This lever should be the gear stick of your financial car (i.e. hand on it most of the time!). You always want to be ensuring you're not paying too much for things in your budget.

Cut something out completely

This is the blunt instrument and it works best when used temporarily. Pause the streaming services. Stop takeaway for a few months. Put discretionary spending on ice for a defined period. This is where discipline shows up. No-one stumbles into a deposit while keeping every comfort switched on. Progress comes from choosing what matters most for your future over what feels good in the moment.

Fast-tracking your deposit

A side hustle, or second job, can be a powerful accelerator when you have a clear financial goal and a defined time frame. Most people think progress comes from cutting expenses or waiting for pay rises. Both help, but they are slow. A side hustle adds force. Instead of squeezing your lifestyle harder, you create extra income that's purpose-built for a single outcome. That might be a property deposit (hello!), clearing debt, building a buffer or buying back time later.

From a money perspective, the biggest advantage of a side hustle is that it can be quarantined. Your main income pays for life. Your side hustle pays for progress. When extra money has a job, it sticks. An extra $500 a month directed straight to a deposit can shave years off your timeline. That kind of acceleration is hard to replicate through budgeting alone. You're not just moving faster—you're reducing risk by reaching financial milestones sooner.

A side hustle also creates momentum and optionality. Hitting your deposit goal sooner means fewer years exposed to rising rents, interest rate changes or job uncertainty. It may allow you to enter the property market earlier, upgrade sooner or simply sleep better knowing you have a buffer. Importantly, a side hustle doesn't have to be permanent. It can be seasonal, project-based or time-bound. Many people run one intensely for a year or two, hit the goal, then shut it down. That's not failure. That's the plan working.

> The ultimate warning when getting a second job, a side hustle or doing overtime is that if you use the money for 'stuff' or routine budget line items, you risk getting stuck on the side hustle, second job, overtime train. Not a train you want to be on!

There's also a behavioural truth worth stating plainly. No-one achieves meaningful financial results without hard work and sacrifice. Every deposit story includes trade-offs. Fewer nights on the couch, as you're working back late. Fewer episodes watched. More effort applied with intent. Pouring beers on a school night isn't glamorous, but it works. Great results are rarely comfortable, but they're usually temporary.

The truth is simple. Buying property requires effort, consistency and the willingness to be uncomfortable for a season. No-one gets there by accident. People who succeed worked harder for a period, earned extra income, spent less than their peers and stayed focused when it would have been easier not to. Pull the right levers, protect your savings and the deposit becomes a timeline problem, not a pipe dream.

Saving a deposit

Once the basics are in place—that is, an emergency fund, a buffer account and consumer debt are under control—the focus naturally turns to saving a deposit. For some people, that means starting from scratch. For others, the path is helped along by government schemes, family support or a mix of both. Either way, a deposit isn't a vague idea. It's a number and it has a deadline attached.

Deposit requirements can look very different from one person to the next. Some people need no cash deposit at all because of family support. Others may qualify for a 5 per cent deposit through a government scheme. Some will buy an investment property first and aim for a 10 per cent deposit plus costs. Others will need a much larger amount because of income limits, property price or lender policy. In most cases, saving a deposit takes time and usually involves a period of trade-offs.

The principle is always the same. A deposit goal is simply a dollar amount divided by the number of weeks available or desirable. Once the time frame is clear, saving stops being emotional and starts becoming practical.

Understanding deposit terminology

Before getting into the mechanics of saving, it helps to understand the language that gets thrown around during the buying process. The word 'deposit' is used in different ways and that's where a lot of confusion arises.

Deposit (savings)

This is what most people mean when they talk about a deposit. It's the money being contributed towards the purchase price, usually expressed as a percentage. It's often just called 'savings'. This is also considered the equity that you personally put into the property.

Genuine savings

This is a lending term. Some lenders want to see that part of the contribution has been built up over time, not transferred in at the last minute. This is usually shown through bank statements that demonstrate consistent saving. In some cases, rental payment history can help show savings behaviour, but it doesn't replace the actual cash needed to complete a purchase.

Deposit (contract)

During the buying process, 'deposit' can also refer to the amount paid when contracts are exchanged. This is commonly 10 per cent of the purchase price, even if a high percentage of the property is being borrowed. In some situations, a lower amount can be negotiated, but that needs to be agreed to before contracts are signed.

If cash is not available for the contract deposit, a deposit bond may be an option. This allows the purchase to proceed while covering the deposit amount until settlement. It's a specialised product and should always be assessed with professional advice.

Funds to complete

Funds to complete is the total cash needed to settle the purchase. This includes the deposit contribution plus other costs such as stamp duty, legal fees, inspections and government charges. For some people, this number is small. For others, it's one of the biggest hurdles.

Understanding these distinctions early can save a lot of confusion and last-minute stress.

Setting the savings target

Before locking in a savings target, it's worth having a conversation with a mortgage broker. This isn't about applying for a loan straight away. It's about understanding what a realistic deposit looks like, how much is needed all up to complete a purchase and whether there's any support or concessions that could apply. Having a clear number gives direction. Prices and policies can change, but a starting point allows progress to be tracked and adjusted along the way.

Looking beyond the deposit percentage

Focusing only on the deposit percentage can be misleading. A more useful approach is to look at the total savings goal.

For example:

- Property price: $500 000
- Deposit (5 per cent): $25 000
- Other purchase costs: $7500
- Total savings goal: $32 500

Once the total is clear, it can be broken down into smaller, more manageable targets.

Breaking the goal into weeks

Big numbers feel heavy. Weekly targets make them easier to deal with.

Saving $32 500 looks very different depending on the timeline:

- Over one year, it's around $625 per week
- Over two years, it's around $313 per week
- Over three years, it's around $209 per week.

The challenge doesn't disappear, but it becomes clearer. Clear targets are easier to plan for and stick to. This exercise may put into perspective that your deposit savings could be a 4-year (or more) plan.

Maximising and automating your savings

Saving works best when it happens without constant decision making. Relying on whatever is left at the end of the month rarely produces consistent results.

A simple system usually works best:

- a dedicated high-interest savings account (with a different bank so you don't see it all the time!)
- automatic transfers aligned to your pay cycle
- treating the transfer like a fixed commitment.

Amounts can start small and increase over time. Consistency is far more important than going hard and burning out.

Saving for a deposit doesn't mean life has to stop. It does mean being more intentional for a period of time. This often involves reviewing subscriptions, being more deliberate with discretionary spending and paying attention to everyday purchases. The aim is not deprivation. It is redirection. Small changes, repeated over time, add up. We will talk about another savings option later, the First Home Super Saver scheme (FHSS).

Housing choices and savings speed

Housing is usually the biggest expense, which means it has the biggest impact on how quickly savings grow. People who can reduce rent, even temporarily, often make much faster progress. That might mean living at home, sharing accommodation or choosing a more affordable rental for a defined period. Not everyone has this option, especially families with fixed costs, but when it is available, it can significantly shorten the savings timeline.

Tracking your progress

Progress is easier to maintain when it is visible. This might be done through a spreadsheet, an app or a visual reminder at home. The method doesn't matter nearly as much as making progress easy to see. Milestones are worth acknowledging. Hitting savings benchmarks builds momentum and keeps the goal front of mind.

Buying with a partner

Buying property with a partner adds another layer to the process. It's not just a financial decision. It's a relationship one. There's no single right way to manage money as a couple. Some combine finances completely. Others keep things separate. Many use a shared account for property costs and separate accounts for personal spending. What matters most is that both people understand the system and agree to it. Conversations should cover income, savings, existing debts, spending habits and any outside support. Differences in money attitudes are common and manageable when they are talked about early. Key discussions before buying together include how savings will be contributed, how risk will be handled and how ownership will be structured. Options such as joint tenants or tenants in common have different implications and should be discussed with a conveyancer. (We delve more deeply into joint ownership options in chapter 4.)

It's just as important to agree on how money will be managed after settlement. Clear systems and regular check-ins reduce stress and help prevent small issues from becoming bigger ones.

Effort, consistency and time

Saving a deposit is rarely comfortable. Every successful story includes trade-offs and periods of focused effort. Progress comes from consistency over time, not from getting everything perfect. Property ownership is usually achieved by people who stay focused long enough for their plan to work. With a clear target, a simple structure and patience, the deposit becomes a question of timing rather than possibility.

> Buying your first property is not a race and not buying this year does not mean you are falling behind. Sometimes the smartest move is to pause, prepare and strengthen your position. If your income is unstable, your savings habits are inconsistent, or your life is in the middle of major change, waiting can be a strategic decision rather than a missed opportunity.
>
> The key is intention. Waiting without a plan leads to frustration. Waiting with clear actions leads to progress. Improving savings habits, reducing debt, building a buffer, or getting clarity on your goals all count as forward movement. Not buying yet is only a problem if nothing is changing. If you are actively setting yourself up, you are still very much in the game.

New to Australia?

First of all, welcome. It's so great you're here. Moving to a new country is a big step. Buying your first home here can feel overwhelming, especially without family on the ground to help guide the process. The good news is that Australia does allow permanent residents, and in some cases other visa holders, to buy property. With the right advice early, the process can be far smoother than many people expect.

The first step is understanding the rules that apply to your visa, the types of property you are allowed to buy and what grants or concessions may be available. This is where early advice matters. Speaking with a conveyancer and a mortgage broker upfront helps clarify both the legal and lending requirements at each stage. It is important that both professionals are experienced with visa-related purchases and up to date with current regulations, particularly if one or all buyers are not yet permanent residents.

Temporary visas and permanent residency are treated very differently. Permanent residents are now largely treated the same as citizens when buying property. There could, however, be some government schemes that are only available to citizens. Changes introduced in 2023 gave permanent residents access to the First Home Guarantee scheme and first-home buyer grants, in addition to stamp duty concessions that have been available to permanent residents in many states since 2017.

From a deposit perspective, this can make a significant difference. For an eligible home that falls within price caps and stamp duty thresholds, a permanent resident may be able to buy with as little as a 5 per cent deposit, plus around $5000 in other purchase costs. On a $600 000 home, that could mean getting into the market with roughly $35 000.

It may still be possible to buy property before gaining permanent residency, but the rules are tighter. From a lending perspective, a larger deposit is often required. There may also be restrictions on the type of property that can be purchased, such as being limited to new builds, along with additional taxes or the need for approval from the Foreign Investment Review Board. A conveyancer or solicitor will guide buyers through these requirements and help avoid costly mistakes.

Gordana and Jordon were registered nurses who had come to Australia on a skilled work visa. Rach's team met with them in early 2023 and at that stage they had $35 000 in savings and wanted to know how to enter the Australian property market. Gordana had her Permanent Resident Visa and Jordon was still on a partner visa. At that stage the deposit they needed to get in at $750 000 purchase was about $80 000 as they had to be citizens to buy under the federal government's 5% Deposit Scheme. They embarked on a two-year savings plan to get to the deposit goal of $80 000. By July 2023, when the rules changed and permanent residents could qualify for the scheme, they had saved $50 000. They were able to buy at $750 000 with $42 500 using a combination of the Australian Government 5% Deposit Scheme and state-based stamp duty concessions.

Here are the numbers:

- $750 000: purchase price
- $5000: costs (allows for legal fees, pest and building inspections, etc.)
- $755 000: funds needed to complete the purchase
- $712 500: loan amount (95 per cent lending, using 5% Deposit Scheme, avoiding LMI)
- $42 500: cash contribution needed from Gordana and Jordon

What we can learn:

- Gordana and Jordon had seen a conveyancer and a mortgage broker early on.

(continued)

- They were kept up to date with any important changes that allowed them to get into the market early.
- They had a plan in place that meant if the government scheme change had not taken place they would have entered the market in 2025 rather than 2023.

Dwight and Madison had moved to Australia under Dwight's skilled visa. He became a permanent resident, but Madison was awaiting her permanent resident status and it was at least six months off when they found their dream home. The conveyancer advised that if Madison went on the title for the home, they would be subject to foreign investor tax. They found a lender who was able to use both incomes with only one name on the title.

Timing can also be critical. One client of Rach's from New Zealand was about to exchange on a property when it emerged that, just three weeks later, she would meet the residency threshold for a full stamp duty exemption. Delaying the exchange saved her $37 000. That outcome only happened because the conversation took place before contracts were signed. Her mortgage rate was already competitive, but the real win came from understanding the timing rules.

This is why speaking to a mortgage broker early is so valuable. There's no cost to do so and early conversations can uncover opportunities or risks that are easy to miss when you're only focused on finding a property. Getting advice before it feels urgent can make a meaningful difference to both cost and stress.

Let's walk through some real-life examples of people saving for a deposit.

Emma and Matt saved while renting.

Situation: Renting in the suburbs, paying $450/week

Goal: To save a $60 000 deposit for their first home

Plan: Committed to saving $300/week over four years while renting. They budgeted carefully, cut unnecessary expenses and redirected small windfalls into savings

Outcome: By consistently saving, they reached their $60 000 target without living at home or changing jobs

Takeaway: Steady, consistent savings over time can achieve big goals, even while paying rent.

Ethan lived at home and invested regionally.

Situation: Lived at home during university and the first two years of work

Savings: $40 000 in a one-year term deposit (earning 4.35 per cent)

Goal: Build a total $90 000 deposit for a property in regional Queensland

Plan: Save $480/week for two years while continuing to live at home

Outcome: Hit the deposit target within two years by delaying moving out and cutting back on travel

Takeaway: Living at home can fast-track your savings and help you buy property sooner

(continued)

Karen and Dylan planned for an investment property.

Situation: Rented in the CBD, planned to buy a regional investment property

Goal: $600 000 property with 10 per cent deposit + stamp duty → $90 000 total savings

Plan: To save over two years, using Karen's sales commissions and Dylan's optional Saturday work

Outcome: Achieved deposit without compromising long-term financial stability

Takeaway: Extra income streams and careful budgeting make larger deposits achievable.

ooo

Megan and Jess used government schemes to their advantage.

Situation: Two kids, $17 000 savings, previously over income threshold for the Australian Government 5% Deposit Scheme

Goal: $850 000 property, 5 per cent deposit + reduced stamp duty + other costs = $57 500 total

Plan: To save $500/week, sell/downgrade a car, use 'genuine savings' from rental statements and family gift

Outcome: Able to reach deposit target in months instead of years

Takeaway: Staying informed about government incentives can dramatically shorten your savings timeline as income caps were removed at the end of 2025 for this scheme.

Caitlyn displayed persistence and sacrifice for a home.

Situation: Single mother, saved $25 000 inheritance, added $15 000 while studying

Goal: Home for her and her daughter. Needed $100 000 deposit + emergency fund. Deposit needed to be so large as her maximum loan amount was low due to her income

Plan: To move back in with parents, save $500/week, work overtime, strategic planning with a broker

Outcome: Bought $495 000 townhouse in January 2023; mortgage payments lower than previous rent, property increased in value to $600 000 by 2025

Takeaway: Long-term persistence, strategic planning and temporary sacrifices can lead to property ownership even in tight markets.

Other purchase costs and considerations

When people ask about the 'other costs' of buying a property, what they are usually asking about is stamp duty. For most buyers, stamp duty is the single biggest cost outside the deposit. Stamp duty is a state-based tax calculated on a sliding scale and the rules change regularly.

Thresholds move, concessions come and go, and what applied a few years ago may no longer apply today. Because of that, we wanted to avoid listing fixed dollar amounts as definitive. Make sure you always confirm current figures with your state-based government website, conveyancer and mortgage broker.

As a rule of thumb, any stamp duty exemptions or concessions for first-home buyers are tied to living in the property (for a period of time within the first 12 months). If you are a first-home buyer purchasing an investment property that you do not live in, those concessions generally don't apply. This is a common misunderstanding and can materially change how much cash you need. It's important not to discount buying an investment property as your first home just because you have to pay stamp duty. Overall, it could be a more favourable outcome for you than buying a place that might cost more and that you live in, just to avoid some stamp duty. *Remember:* your 'why' must come first.

It's also important to note that the examples shown are for established homes. Many states offer higher incentives or different concessions for newly built properties and these rules change frequently. A good mortgage broker will check what applies at the time you are actively considering your options.

Beyond stamp duty, there are a range of additional costs that vary depending on your state, the property type, whether the purchase is owner-occupied or an investment, and the professionals you engage. LMI isn't listed here because it's highly lender specific and should always be calculated by your mortgage broker. Their job is to minimise or avoid it where possible and we cover this in detail in chapter 3.

As a broad planning rule, many buyers allow around $5000 for general purchase costs, excluding stamp duty. This is not a precise number, but it is a practical placeholder that prevents under-budgeting. Typical costs include conveyancing or legal fees, building and pest inspections, loan application or package fees, government mortgage registration fees and title transfer fees. Some of these vary significantly by state and purchase price, particularly title transfer fees at higher property values.

Finally, remember that purchasing the property is not the same as being ready to live in it. If you're moving into the home, you'll also need funds for moving costs, utility connections, initial maintenance and home contents insurance.

Insurance costs in particular can vary widely by property and location, so it's smart to check insurance premiums before you buy. You might not decide to buy an investment property in far north Queensland (hint: cyclones) or parts of northern New South Wales (hint: chronic flooding) as the costs of insurance make the deal dead before you start! This could be a reason why you may choose to rent in these areas and invest elsewhere if you're strategic with your life and money goals. While these aren't technical costs, they are very real cash outflows that catch buyers off guard if they're not planned for upfront.

Start with this...

To make the most out of this chapter, consider the following:

* What financial foundations do you need to build before you buy your first property?
* Which of the four budget levers do you need to pull to achieve your goal of buying your first property?
* How can you level up in your career to improve your earning capabilities?
* Have you fallen into any financial traps? What behaviours need to stop, and what changes need to be made?

For a more in-depth explanation of the sound financial house, follow the QR code on page 300 to see an explainer video.

3

Understanding home loans

For many first-home buyers, the biggest question is often, 'Where do I start?' We believe the best place to begin your journey is with an experienced and trusted mortgage broker.

Buying your first home is exciting, but understanding how lending works is what truly empowers you. This chapter breaks down loan types and gives you a clear starting point. If you begin here, by the time you start inspecting homes you'll understand what you can borrow, be pre-approved, have a set budget and be ready to negotiate with confidence.

A mortgage is likely the biggest loan you'll ever take out, so it's worth knowing as much as possible before signing on the dotted line. Every bank and lender has different rules, rates and policies and assesses income differently. Some participate in government schemes; some don't. Some offer strong parental-guarantee options or special deals for certain professionals; others don't. The days of walking into a bank and asking for a loan are long gone and with the sheer number of lenders available, you wouldn't want to. This is exactly where a mortgage broker can be valuable and ensure you plan and complete your lending journey successfully.

The figures and examples in this chapter may vary depending on the lending environment. Rates, bank calculations and policies shift regularly. The key is to work closely with a mortgage broker so that you understand your personal lending position clearly.

What do mortgage brokers do and how are they paid?

Great mortgage brokers do far more than simply compare loans. They can evaluate all your available lending scenarios, compare lenders that suit your situation, help you determine the right strategy, manage your application through to approval and look after you post-settlement to ensure your mortgage remains competitive. It's a big role, and one that spans your entire buying journey, so choosing the right broker is essential.

Here's one of the best parts: you typically *don't pay* for their service. Most mortgage brokers are free to the client. The bank or lender pays the broker a commission when your loan settles without increasing the rate you pay. This is because the broker has effectively done the legwork for the lender, saving them internal costs such as staff salaries, marketing and branch overheads.

A good broker should also save you time and money by guiding you through the buying process and helping you make informed, strategic decisions. It's genuinely a win-win.

The Mortgage and Finance Association of Australia (MFAA) has data that says well over 75 per cent of residential home loans are obtained through a mortgage broker.

It's usually for one of these reasons:

- *Choice:* brokers have access to dozens of banks and lenders. Some have a panel of up to 60, though most only use 10 to 20 regularly.
- *Experience:* brokers deal with lenders daily. They know which ones will suit your situation and strategy.
- *Avoiding pitfalls:* structuring mistakes like fixing an entire loan or using redraw on an investment loan can cost you thousands. A broker helps you avoid such mistakes.
- *Ongoing relationship:* your broker doesn't disappear after settlement. They're there to answer questions along the way and will review your lending regularly to ensure your loan remains at a competitive rate. If a refinance is needed down the track, you keep the same point of contact. They're someone you can return to when you're ready for your next purchase.

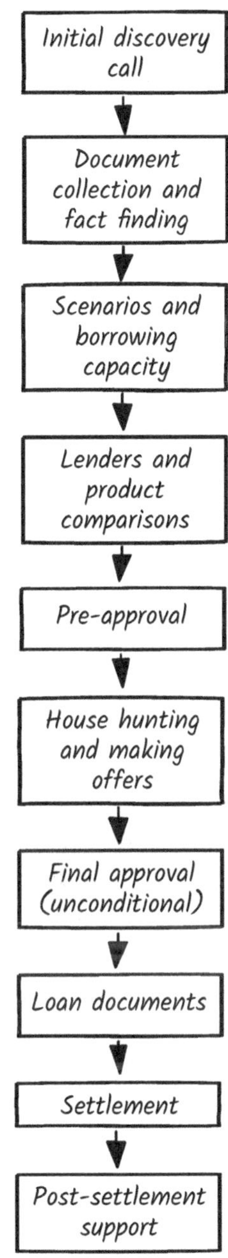

Figure 3.1: a typical home-loan process

When choosing a broker, look for someone who explains the buying and lending process clearly (see figure 3.1). Some brokers specialise in first-home buyers and are happy to spend more time with you upfront, which is exactly what many first-time buyers need. Don't be afraid to ask questions. Be intentional about who you choose and why.

Another important factor is experience and training. Unfortunately, the entry level for the mortgage broking industry is low. You want to see a few years of experience with decent loan volumes before taking advice from someone. Lending scenarios vary widely and without experience, a broker may not be the asset you hoped for. Do your research, check their background and ask questions like:

- How long have you been a mortgage broker?
- How many loans did you settle in the past 12 months and across how many lenders?
- What does your post-settlement service look like?
- Who do I speak to if you're unavailable?
- Do you work with many first-home buyers?
- Will you spend time with me upfront as I prepare to buy?
- Do you have a support team?
- Are there any costs for your service, either on the way in or post settlement, such as if I refinance in a year?

Let's step through what it's like to engage a mortgage broker and what you can expect from the process.

1 Initial discovery call

This is your starting point. Think of it as a strategy conversation. The broker will ask you about:

- how much you have saved for a deposit
- your income
- whether you have family help available
- your time frame: Are you looking to buy now or are you on a journey?
- whether you're buying to live in or invest
- your goals.

This call helps the broker sense what's realistic right now. It's also an opportunity for you to ask questions about the broker and their process before you go down the track of supplying personal information.

You might move straight on to the next step or this call may only be for you to get some plans in place. Some people stay here for months (or even years) while they save or plan, and that's fine.

Generally, you move to step 2 once you're ready to start working things out more formally.

2 Document collection and fact finding

This is where things become more detailed.

A fact find is a formal questionnaire that captures your full financial picture. It includes:

- income (salary, bonuses, overtime, commission, other income sources)

- living expenses
- existing debts (HELP, car loans, credit cards, buy-now-pay-later balances)
- savings and assets
- future plans that may impact your loan.

You will also be asked to upload documents via a secure portal. These may include:

- Identification
- recent payslips and payment summaries or tax returns
- bank statements
- loan statements
- savings history.

This is not about judging you; it's about accuracy. Not all of this information will go to a bank or lender. However, the mortgage broker needs all of this to determine which lenders will (or won't) suit your situation.

This gives the broker a clear financial picture. You might sign a privacy consent so the broker can hold your information and complete a credit check. It's important that your broker has all the information upfront so that their advice is accurate. Without it, they can't give you recommendations or information.

Top tip: Be completely honest and upfront with your broker, they need to know all of the information to help guide you.

A note on credit scores

At this stage the broker will run a credit check on you with one of the credit bureaus in Australia. It will give them a full report with information on your current or previous credit enquiries or loans. Some lenders have rules around people's credit history and this may impact which lender the broker recommends.

A credit check:

* shows lenders how reliable you have been with past lending
* helps the broker choose a lender who may be more forgiving of an issue, if there has been one
* prevents surprises later in the process.

A good broker will explain your credit file and talk you through any concerns. If you have concerns about your credit file, let the broker know; they will work with you to find a solution.

Just to bust a myth, this is less about the 'credit score' you may have received with an online search or what the broker receives, and more about your credit profile. Credit scores can change among credit bureaus in Australia (of which there are three main ones). There's no standardised scoring system, which is why it's more about your overall profile than a 'credit score' or number.

3 Scenarios and borrowing capacity

This is one of the most valuable parts of working with a mortgage broker, especially for first-home buyers.

Some buyers know exactly what they want. For example, 'I want to borrow $500 000 to buy a $700 000 home'. In this case a broker could go straight to lender comparisons after your borrowing capacity has been assessed.

But most first-home buyers aren't sure yet. This is where scenarios are essential. Common scenario questions include:

- How much can I borrow if I buy a property to live in?
- What if I stay living with my family?
- What if I keep some cash aside?
- How much is LMI if I have a low deposit amount?
- What if I choose a shorter loan term?

Your broker will run as many scenarios as needed. Step 4 doesn't begin until you choose which path you want to follow.

4 Lenders and product comparisons

Once your scenario, purpose, loan amount and estimated purchase price are defined, your broker compares lenders based on:

- your borrowing capacity
- how much they will lend you
- how they will assess your income type

- desired product features (offset, basic, flexibility, etc.)
- interest rates
- processing time frames
- policy fit for your situation
- LMI costs, if applicable.

Your broker's expertise matters here because not all banks assess income or risk the same way.

When you choose a lender, you sign that lender's privacy form so that your broker can submit your application.

5 Pre-approval

At this stage your broker packages and submits your application. Some lenders approve quickly; others may take weeks. Time frames are a key comparison factor and brokers generally know how quickly a bank will move to get your pre-approval sorted. Once approved, you receive conditional pre-approval, typically valid for 90 days and extendable. So if 90 days pass and you haven't locked in a property, you can ask your broker to extend it for another 90 days.

Pre-approval is a conditional 'yes'. It confirms the lender is prepared to lend subject to:

- no major changes in your situation
- the property meeting their criteria
- possible other conditions, which your broker will explain to you.

It is important to let your broker know of any changes to your financial situation from here on. Changing jobs or taking out a car loan, for example, can make your pre-approval invalid.

6 House hunting and making offers

Looking for the right home is where the fun begins. (We go through this in more detail in chapters 7 and 8.)

When making an offer, your broker supports your conveyancer with borrowing details and contract clauses.

7 Final approval (unconditional)

Once you secure a property, your broker sends the contract of sale and valuation to the lender. If anything has changed since pre-approval, or if timing/product differences arise, your broker may suggest switching lenders at this stage. Pre-approval is only an offer; unconditional approval locks everything in.

8 Loan documents

This is when you receive your loan documents and review them with your broker. You set up direct debits and open any required accounts or offsets.

Now is the time to ask questions about your loan and how it works. Nothing is too trivial here; you need to understand all of the contracts and what you are signing.

9 Settlement

At settlement, your broker coordinates with your conveyancer and lender to ensure everything is ready. Once settlement has taken place, the property is legally yours.

10 Post-settlement support

A good broker checks in after settlement and reviews your loan annually, especially after fixed rates expire or when market changes may affect your loan. They can negotiate your rate or refinance if needed.

ooo

Mortgage brokers aren't just there to get you a loan. They are there to help you make smart, informed decisions that support your future. If you feel rushed, confused or pressured, that's a sign to pause and rethink your choice of broker. The right broker will bring clarity, not chaos.

Things don't always run perfectly, and that's normal. A bank might make a simple admin error, like spelling your name incorrectly; a small blip on your credit file may raise questions; or a valuation could be delayed, meaning you need an extension on your cooling-off period or finance clause. These moments can feel stressful, especially as a first-home buyer. While your broker can't always prevent these issues, their role is to guide you through them, explain what's happening, manage the moving parts and help keep the process on track so you're not navigating it alone.

A good mortgage broker should feel like a guide, not a sales person. The best brokers slow the process down, ask better questions and actually care about where you're headed—not just whether your loan gets approved. They take the time to understand your 'why', explain things in plain English and show you options—not just tell you they can get you a loan.

(continued)

A great broker will talk you through different scenarios, explain the risks as well as the benefits and help you structure a loan that works for you not only today, but as your life changes. You should walk away feeling clearer, calmer and more confident—not rushed or confused. Most importantly, a good broker is honest. If you're not ready, they will tell you. That kind of advice is worth more than a quick approval.

Broker red flags:

* They push one lender without explaining why.
* They don't explain LMI, fees or long-term implications.
* They rush you.
* They're not interested in helping you on the journey before you're ready.
* They talk about maximum loan amounts, not you and your budget.
* They avoid questions or make you feel silly for asking them.
* They don't ask about your future plans.
* They're not listed as a broker with the Australian Securities & Investment Commission (ASIC).
* They don't give you a credit proposal with lender comparisons before you choose a lender.

The majority of brokers are in this business to genuinely help people, but like all industries there are a few bad eggs. There are also some who become brokers before being adequately trained and may give poor advice. And there are those who join the industry quickly and then leave just as quickly, abandoning their clients with no support. Beware of any signs that appear concerning.

When choosing a mortgage broker, as well as checking Google reviews (read the reviews—don't just look at the stars), you should ask them:

* who you can talk to when they're not available. Do they have a team around them?
* about their post-settlement process. Will they review your loan and ensure you're on the best rate? (Do their Google reviews support these statements?)
* how long they have been a broker and their experience in the finance industry.

Your first home loan isn't just a transaction, it's a foundation. The right broker helps you build it properly.

When should you speak with a mortgage broker?

The earlier, the better. Even if you're 12 to 24 months away from buying, a broker can help you map out a plan, understand your borrowing capacity and become 'purchase ready'. If your goal is to own a home, a broker can help you reverse-engineer that goal into actionable steps.

Common early-stage conversations include:

- How much deposit do I need?
- How much should I be saving each month?
- What price range is realistic for me?

- When will I be ready to buy?
- Should I pay down debt?
- Should I live at home longer or rent?

Use this time to improve your position: update your savings pattern, reduce expenses, improve your credit score, strategically pay down debts, have your accounts in order or build a stronger employment history. A good broker will guide you through this.

The purpose of running scenarios

Many first-home buyers assume they need to buy a home to live in. But that isn't always the only, or the best, strategy. This is where scenario planning—and reflecting on your 'why' statement—becomes incredibly valuable. Running scenarios with a mortgage broker shows you what you can achieve, and the various ways to get there. Examples of common scenarios include:

- *Buying to live in*
  - What can you borrow?
  - How much deposit do you need?
  - What will your repayments look like?
- *Renting where you want to live, and buying where you can afford*
  This can widen your options significantly. Your first property doesn't have to be your forever home.

- *Staying with family temporarily*
  This can reduce living expenses, improve savings or increase borrowing capacity.
- *Maximising government grants*
  - What's possible with the First Home Guarantee?
  - Do you qualify for stamp duty concessions?
  - How do these incentives change your budget?
- *Buying with a partner, sibling or friend*
  - What's the best structure?
  - Who's responsible for what portion?
  - What happens later if plans change?
- *Building or buying off-the-plan*
  Different fees, valuations and timelines apply.

Can you see how varied these scenarios are? There's no one-size-fits-all and that's exactly why scenarios are important. Once you've chosen your direction, your broker can match lenders to your strategy.

Borrowing capacity

A common question is 'How much can I borrow?' The answer is different depending on your situation and what assistance you may have available, either from the government, your family or lending guidelines. Figure 3.2 (overleaf) breaks it down in a simple but generalised way.

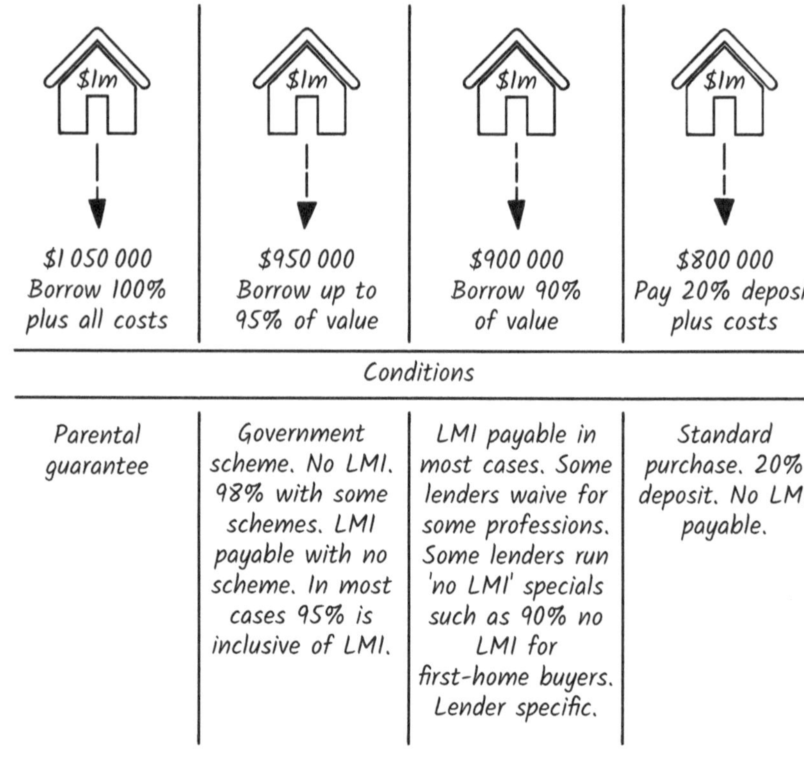

Figure 3.2: working out how much you can borrow

What 'borrowing capacity' actually means

Borrowing capacity is the amount a lender is willing to loan you based on income, living expenses, debts, credit history, dependants, employment stability, the interest rate buffer (or 'stress test'—we'll get to that soon) and lender policy.

A broker compares multiple lenders because each lender calculates capacity differently. One lender may offer $620 000, while another may offer $750 000 based on the same income.

This is because banks have different assessment tools, rules and policies—and these change regularly. Which is why running your borrowing capacity through only one lender often leads to confusion or disappointment. Brokers help you see the full landscape of lending available and can line you up with the optimum lender for your situation.

If you're paying rent, use that to your advantage. You already know the weekly amount your budget can handle.

Tell your mortgage broker your preferred repayment: 'I can comfortably pay $X per week in rent. What can I borrow at that repayment rate?'

Why the stress test matters

When lenders assess how much you can borrow, they don't just look at today's interest rate. Instead, they apply a buffer, usually around 3 per cent higher than the current rate, to make sure you could still afford your repayments if rates rise in the future. This is called a 'stress test'.

For example, if the current interest rate is 5 per cent, the bank might calculate your repayments as if the rate were 8 per cent. The goal isn't to trick you or limit your borrowing unfairly; it's to protect you from taking on more debt than you can realistically manage if interest rates go up. Understanding the stress test helps you see why your borrowing limit might be lower than you expected and why adding a buffer to your budget is important.

Comparing loans

When you're comparing home loans, you can't just look at any two interest rates side by side. Every loan is designed for a specific type of borrower and a specific situation, so the only fair comparison is between comparable products.

This means the loans should be for the same purpose (for example, living in the home vs investing), have the same type of repayments, include similar features, have a similar LVR and both be either fixed or variable. If these features don't match, the comparison won't tell you anything useful.

A low interest rate doesn't necessarily mean it's the best loan for you or that you'll even be eligible for it. Some loans are only offered to people with very low LVRs, specific job types or certain income structures. Others are only available to refinancers and not first-home buyers.

This is why looking at headlines about interest rates online can be misleading: the rate might look amazing, but it may not apply to your situation, your deposit size or the type of loan you need.

Why pre-approval matters

A pre-approval is basically the bank saying, 'Based on what we've seen so far, we're comfortable lending you up to $XXX'. It's not a final 'yes', but it's a strong early indication. Pre-approval confirms:

- the lender has assessed your documents
- you meet their lending criteria
- your borrowing capacity is acceptable
- your application is conditionally approved for a set amount.

While it isn't unconditional approval, it does give you the confidence to start making offers because you know roughly what the bank is prepared to lend you. It can also help you compete more effectively against other buyers. Many agents take pre-approved buyers more seriously and some won't genuinely consider an offer unless pre-approval is in place, especially when two offers are close. In that sense, pre-approval can give you a real edge.

Understanding LMI

If you're saving for your first-home deposit you've probably heard the term Lenders Mortgage Insurance (LMI). It's one of those terms that sound scary and expensive, and a lot of buyers don't come face to face with the term until they are staring at their loan contract. Some people see it as a negative, believing that avoiding the cost is better than the opportunity cost of getting into the market.

In chapter 4, we'll unpack some national schemes that can help you avoid LMI. Some lenders will waive LMI for certain professionals, and parental assistance can also help. We'll explore strategies to remove or reduce LMI shortly, but first let's find out exactly what LMI is.

What is LMI?

LMI is an insurance policy that the bank takes out against you not being able to make repayments. It protects the *lender* — not you — in case the lender incurs a loss.

Borrowing terms such as 'LVR' (Loan-to-Value Ratio) are common when referring to LMI. LVR is calculated by dividing the loan amount by the value of the property. Here's how to work it out:

Loan amount ÷ value of property = LVR

- *Example 1:* $800 000 ÷ $1 000 000 = 80 per cent (LVR is 80 per cent if you borrow $800 000 on $1 million)

- *Example 2:* $950 000 ÷ $1 000 000 = 95 per cent (LVR is 95 per cent if you borrow $950 000 on $1 million)

Understanding LVR is also important when we discuss ways to use the equity in your home (later in this chapter).

Okay, so back to LMI. Here's the hard part: *you* pay the insurance premium. Many people believe it protects them, but it only protects the lender (however, it can help you get into the market sooner). You do need to protect yourself in other ways — like home insurance and income protection — which we address in chapter 10.

LMI is generally payable if your deposit is less than 20 per cent of the property value. Banks and lenders prefer low-risk loans. If you save a 20 per cent deposit, you're considered low risk because the bank believes if you stop repaying the loan, they can recover their costs by selling the property. Borrowing more — meaning a higher LVR — increases the bank's risk. If you default and the bank has to sell, they could lose money. To manage this, a third party (sometimes the bank itself) insures the loan so they won't lose money if this happens.

LMI isn't payable with incentives like the government's 5% Deposit Scheme, but avoiding LMI through these programs comes with restrictions on the property (more on this in chapter 4). Your mortgage broker can discuss scenarios to work out what's best for you.

Many first-home buyers choose to buy with less than a 20 per cent deposit because:

- property prices may rise faster than they can save
- waiting longer may push them out of their desired area
- the cost of LMI may be lower than the cost of waiting.

Your broker can calculate different LMI scenarios so you can weigh up the pros and cons.

How much does LMI cost?

LMI is a one-off fee that you may need to pay when you take out a home loan. Sometimes it can be added to the loan and sometimes you have to pay it upfront. When discussing scenarios, your mortgage broker will talk about a 'base loan amount' and a 'capped loan amount' if you are capitalising your LMI premium into your loan (that is, adding it to the loan amount). However, you can't 'cap' this premium into the loan if it exceeds the lender's maximum lending policy.

For example, if a lender has a maximum lending percentage of 95 per cent and you have a 5 per cent deposit, you can't cap the insurance premium in because you're already at the lender's maximum LVR. However, if you're borrowing, say, 88 per cent of the loan amount, you can add the insurance premium to your loan as long as the LVR remains under 95 per cent.

The amount you pay will depend on three things:

- your loan amount
- your LVR
- the bank or lender, and potentially their insurer.

The premium can vary greatly. For example, borrowing 86 per cent on a loan amount of $500 000 may cost $2000 in LMI, whereas borrowing 95 per cent with the same loan amount could be $15 000. Likewise, an LVR of 95 per cent on a $1 000 000 loan amount may be as high as $40 000.

To complicate this further, all banks have different scales they use to calculate LMI and the premium so your mortgage broker will not only be comparing lenders' rates and loan features—they will also consider whether LMI is payable and if so how much. The LMI premium may be a determining factor in which lender you choose.

Ways to reduce LMI

Even if you don't have a 20 per cent deposit saved, there are a few legitimate ways to reduce or avoid LMI:

- Save more deposit
- A family guarantee (see chapter 4)
- Government schemes (see chapter 4)
- Professional waivers can apply for certain professions. They will vary depending on the lender, and they change regularly, so it's best to check with a broker before you pay LMI because once it's paid you can't get it back
- Sometimes lenders run specials, such as '85 per cent no LMI' for first-home buyers; or '90 per cent no LMI' for emergency service workers. From time to time they may run reduced LMI for low-risk clients (such as those with healthy credit profiles). Your broker will investigate these and establish whether you're eligible.

If you're buying a property as an investment, the LMI is tax deductible (not upfront, but spread out). This is great if you're buying your first home as an investment, and can also be handy down the track when using the equity in your home to buy your next one because you can use strategies to ensure the LMI is on the tax-deductible loan.

Do I need LMI?

You're trying to save to get into the market, not add extra costs. So LMI can feel frustrating because you have to pay it but you don't benefit from it directly. However, it also opens the door for buyers who don't have decades of savings behind them to get into the market sooner rather than later.

An important thing to remember is that LMI isn't a penalty—it's a tool.

Government incentives at a glance

There are several government incentives available, and they change regularly. Your eligibility will depend on income, purchase price, deposit size and citizenship.

A broker can explain options like:

- the First Home Guarantee
- the Family Home Guarantee
- regional schemes
- stamp duty concessions
- first-home buyer grants (where applicable).

These schemes can reduce your required deposit significantly, sometimes down to as little as 2 per cent deposit with no LMI. We'll dive into more detail on these in chapter 4, so sit tight.

The two main factors lenders look at

When you're borrowing for your first home, two things matter most:

1. *Your income, expenses and debts*
    - *Income:* your salary plus any additional income streams, such as overtime, bonuses, commissions, rental income and side hustles

- *Expenses:*
    - living expenses (food, fuel, utilities, childcare, insurance, etc.)
    - existing loan repayments
    - subscriptions
    - school fees
- *Debts:*
    - personal loans
    - car loans
    - credit card limits (not balances!)
    - buy-now-pay-later accounts
    - HELP debt.

Your income impacts how much you can borrow from the lender (known as *servicing*) and also how much of your own income you personally feel comfortable putting towards a mortgage each month.

Property in action

Take a moment to do a self-assessment of your income, expenses and debts. Even a pen and paper, or a note on your phone is a great place to start. This information can be shown to your mortgage broker to get the conversation about lending started.

2. *Your deposit*

   As we've seen, the money you contribute upfront when buying a property is one of the biggest factors affecting how much you can borrow. A larger deposit usually means a smaller loan, less risk for the lender and a better chance of avoiding LMI. But bigger isn't always better. Saving a large deposit takes time, and while you're saving, property prices may keep rising. That's why finding the right balance matters.

   There's no single answer to how much deposit you will need because everyone's situation is different.

Let's walk through an example to show you how a cash deposit works in the real world. We'll assume:

- you need a *10 per cent deposit*
- you want to buy a property for $700 000
- your purchase costs (legal fees, pest and building inspection reports etc.) will total around $5000
- the stamp duty of $25 912 (in NSW) was waived as you are a first-home buyer living in New South Wales.

Your required contribution becomes:

- *Deposit:* $70 000 (10 per cent of $700 000)
- *Costs:* $5000
- *Total contribution needed:* $75 000

However, you probably don't want to empty your bank account completely. Having a *cash buffer or emergency fund* is wise. Let's assume you want a buffer of $17 000.

That means your *total savings goal* is $92 000.

A buffer amount is personal. Some people are comfortable with $5000; others want $30 000 or more. Choose what suits your situation and comfort level.

Turning the deposit into a savings goal

Once you know your deposit target, the whole process becomes far more manageable. Saving a large deposit can feel impossibly hard when you look at it as one number, but breaking it down into smaller amounts over time makes it realistic and much easier to commit to. Most people find saving far simpler when they have a clear goal in mind and contribute consistently, even in small amounts. If you've ever saved for a car or a holiday, you know how motivating a well-defined goal can be. Saving for a home deposit works the same way.

Let's consider a savings example based on a $92 000 deposit goal:

- *Saving:* $300 per week
- *Time frame:* 5 years
- *Interest rate:* 4 per cent

After 5 years:

- $78 000 would come from your own savings
- $8310 would come from interest earned
- Total: $86 310.
  (does not factor in tax paid on interest, for illustration purposes only)

Ideas for saving a deposit:

* Move back home to reduce or eliminate rent.
* Cut expenses or restructure your budget.
* Pick up extra income, a side hustle or a second job.
* Set up automatic transfers into a high-interest savings account.
* Avoid lifestyle inflation as your income increases.

We'll explore more practical strategies and hacks to help you enter the market in chapter 4.

Due to the compounding effect of interest building up, you'll notice interest grows more significantly in years 3, 4 and 5, because your savings balance has grown.

Car loans: A cautionary tale

Before we move on, we want to touch on the topic of car loans. Aussies love cars. Glen loves cars too. But we need to have a quick chat about how to have a car you love and still set up mortgage lending effectively.

Something happens when you step into a dealership that makes perfectly rational adults think, 'Yep, I definitely need the upgraded wheels and the panoramic sunroof'. Cars are fun and practical but they're also giant money sponges if you're not careful. We prefer to pay cash for cars: it's neater, cleaner, no strings, no interest, no repayments.

You have a choice: you either pay cash, or you borrow money. Borrowing can be totally fine, as long as you keep the loan term short

(Glen suggests a four-year term), avoid balloon payments, bring a decent deposit (even up to 20 per cent of the car value) and most importantly, don't buy more car than your budget can genuinely handle. These are handy tips for your budget and financial life, regardless of whether a home loan is on the horizon or not.

But if you choose to borrow money, don't overlook this: *any car loan you take out directly affects how much you can borrow for a home*. Lenders count the *full repayment* when crunching your borrowing capacity.

Let's look at a novated lease example. You might be surprised at how much a 'little' monthly car payment can shrink your home-loan potential.

Kyle and Gemma earn $90 000 each and plan to buy a property together. Kyle has a novated car lease costing $1240 per month. They have no other debts and no children. Here's how the car lease affects their borrowing:

Scenario	Borrowing power
Gemma alone	$500 000
Kyle alone (with car lease)	$340 000
Kyle alone (no car lease)	$500 000
Kyle + Gemma (with car lease)	$815 000
Kyle + Gemma (no car lease)	$980 000

Why the difference?

The bank sees the car lease as a long-term financial commitment equivalent to debt. Your income is only part of the lending equation. Debts such as car loans, personal loans, credit cards and leases can dramatically reduce your borrowing power. So think carefully before signing up for any kind of loan.

> **An important rule**
>
> Think carefully before signing up for any kind of loan and speak with your mortgage broker if upgrading your car is imminent, as buying the car first may really impact your home loan prospects. This may also work the other way: if you have cash and a car loan, your broker can work out the difference in borrowing if you have a car loan and more cash saved, or no loan and less cash saved.

Self-employment and borrowing

If you're self-employed and hoping to buy a home, good news: it's absolutely possible. The process just looks a bit different because lenders assess self-employed income in a more detailed way. Sole traders, company directors, contractors and gig-economy workers can all be assessed differently by banks and lenders depending on how their income is earned and documented.

Why self-employed borrowing can feel harder

Many business owners reinvest profits back into their business, claim deductions or have income that fluctuates from year to year. That can make your taxable income look lower on paper than what you actually take home, which sometimes means banks need extra information to understand your real earning capacity. The encouraging part is that self-employed lending today is far more flexible than it was a decade ago.

Lenders have different ways of assessing self-employed borrowers. Some may rely only on your director's wage, while others are comfortable with just one year of tax returns or even two years of assessment notices without full financials. Certain lenders will accept contractor income with only a short trading history and some are even open to using projected income in specific industries. With so many variations among lenders, having a broker who truly understands self-employed lending can make a huge difference in finding the right option for you.

Top tips for the self-employed:

* Tell your accountant if you plan to buy property.
* Don't overspend on vehicles just to minimise tax.
* Keep business and personal accounts separate.
* Get advice early.
* Keep good records.
* Don't be discouraged: the right lender makes all the difference.

When Rach left her bank job to start her business, she borrowed as much as she could *before* leaving her PAYG role. She knew she wouldn't be able to borrow again for two years and there's no greater killer of a business than lack of cash flow. Later, during a year of heavy reinvestment, she couldn't borrow at all. But because she knew this ahead of time, every loan she had was set to interest only, so she knew her repayment amounts wouldn't change. Planning is everything.

Jane and Sylvia were both physiotherapists earning solid incomes. Because of their profession, they were eligible for an LMI waiver, a huge borrowing advantage. On paper, they should have been ideal applicants. But there was one hiccup: Sylvia had only recently become self-employed. She didn't yet have the usual tax returns or long trading history that many lenders prefer, which meant their application couldn't be assessed in the standard way.

The fix

She set up a company, paid herself a salary, kept clean records and created a six-month work history.

Result

Their income was accepted and they were able to borrow what they needed.

Lesson

In self-employed lending, a 'no' often isn't a dead end; it usually just means 'not yet'. With the right plan, timing and structure, the outcome can completely change.

How a HELP debt affects borrowing

A HELP (previously HECS) or study debt is considered a 'good debt' when it comes to borrowing. It's a debt you've taken on to further enhance your earning potential and generally aligns to a more stable career. For this reason a HELP debt doesn't have a negative impact on things like your credit score.

When it comes to borrowing for a mortgage, a HELP debt impacts *serviceability*. Serviceability is based on your rate of repayment at that time rather than the amount of HELP debt you have. If you have, say, a HELP debt of $100 000 and you earn less than the threshold to pay that debt back, there would be no difference to your borrowing capacity because it's calculated on what you actually pay back. As your salary increases over time, so will your HELP debt repayment.

For the majority of first-home buyers, the deposit is the factor that holds them back more than serviceability for the loan so it's always best to check your personal situation with a broker before you make a move such as using cash to pay out a HELP loan. A mortgage broker can model your borrowing capacity both with and without your HELP debt so you can make an informed decision before making a move.

Let's run some scenarios for borrowing capacity both with and without HELP debts. This is done on a standard calculator assuming a 30-year loan term and approximate figures only (which are subject to change).

- *Scenario 1:*
  - Single applicant; no children or other debts; salary: $150 000; HELP debt: $10 000.
  - With no HELP debt, this applicant could borrow $920 000.
  - With the HELP debt, their maximum borrowing capacity is $715 000.

As this is a single applicant in the highest bracket for HELP repayments, the debt has a large impact on their borrowing capacity.

- *Scenario 2:*
  - Single applicant; no children or other debts; salary: $80 000; HELP debt: $100 000.
  - With no HELP debt, this applicant could borrow $450 000.
  - With the HELP debt, their maximum borrowing capacity is $400 000.

There isn't a big difference due to the smaller amount of HELP debt repayable on their salary.

- *Scenario 3:*
    - Couple; salaries are $80 000 (applicant 1) and $110 000 (applicant 2); no other debts or dependants.
    - With no HELP debt, this couple could borrow $1 050 000.
    - Maximum loan amount when applicant 1 has a HELP debt: $1 010 000.
    - Maximum loan amount when both applicants have HELP debts: $920 000.

As you can see, for a couple in this lower income bracket, even though their starting loan amounts are similar to scenario 1, having two HELP debts reduces their borrowing capacity significantly. Just to make things even more confusing some banks or lenders will ignore HELP debt if there is a certain time left to pay it off. It can even increase your borrowing capacity as a result so before you pay off HELP debt check in with a broker.

Again, see how helpful scenarios are!

> Janine spent four years aggressively paying off her HELP debt, assuming it would affect her borrowing capacity so much that she wouldn't be able to get a loan. When she then purchased a home, she realised she could have borrowed enough *four years earlier*, even with the HELP debt. Those four years of rising property prices cost her more than the HELP debt ever would have. As for car loans, if you have HELP debt and cash saved, speak to your broker about an appropriate strategy before you take action.

Interest rates explained

Interest rates influence almost everything about your home loan: how much you repay each month, how much you can borrow and even your long-term financial comfort. When interest rates rise, your repayments rise; when they fall, so do your repayments.

In Australia, interest rates are heavily influenced by decisions made by the Reserve Bank of Australia (RBA). The RBA sets the 'cash rate', which acts as the main driver for every bank's borrowing costs. When the RBA changes the cash rate — which you will hear about in the news — banks and lenders usually adjust their own interest rates soon after.

But the cash rate isn't the only factor that affects interest rates. Banks also consider their own funding costs, how competitive the market is and broader economic conditions. All of this flows through to the rate you're offered as a first-home buyer. So while the RBA sets the tone, each lender ultimately chooses the exact rate they apply to your mortgage and that's what determines whether your repayments move up or down.

When you take out a home loan, your interest rate usually comes in one of two forms: *fixed* or *variable*. Each behaves differently as rates rise and fall.

Fixed rates

A fixed rate locks in your interest rate and your repayments for a set period, usually one to five years. This gives you certainty: no matter what the RBA does, your monthly repayments stay the same. For many first-home buyers, that stability is invaluable when you're juggling a new budget. But fixed loans come with trade-offs worth understanding:

- *Less flexibility:* most fixed loans don't offer an offset account.
- *Break fees:* if you sell, refinance or need to make major changes to your loan during the fixed term, you may face significant break costs. These fees are based on the bank's economic loss, which means they can't tell you the exact amount upfront. The longer the remaining fixed period and the lower variable rates have dropped, the higher the break fee can be.
- *Limits on extra repayments:* some fixed loans cap how much extra you can pay each year or block lump-sum payments altogether.

Because of these limits, many borrowers choose a *split loan*: part fixed, part variable. This gives you a measure of certainty while still allowing some flexibility for extra repayments or using an offset on the variable portion. The only drawback a split can't avoid, however, is break fees on the fixed component if your plans change.

To put the impact of break fees into perspective: the largest break fee Rach has seen was $43 000 across two properties when a couple was forced to sell after separating. They locked in when rates were higher; rates dropped soon after and the break cost was substantial.

None of this is to scare you off fixing, but to make sure you fully understand the commitment. Many homeowners are caught off-guard simply because no-one explained the implications clearly upfront.

Before fixing, ask yourself:

- Do I expect my living situation to stay stable for the next one to five years?
- Might I need to sell, refinance or make changes to the loan in that time?

- How important is repayment certainty to me right now?
- Am I comfortable potentially paying more if variable rates fall to lower than my fixed rate percentage?

People who fix usually value certainty above chasing savings. If stability matters most and your plans are unlikely to shift, fixing can be a great option.

Variable rates

Variable rates move up and down over time, usually following changes in the RBA cash rate and each lender's own pricing decisions. This means your repayment amount isn't locked in: it can rise when rates rise and fall when rates fall. For some buyers, that unpredictability can feel uncomfortable. For others, it's a worthwhile trade-off for the flexibility that a variable loan provides.

Flexibility is the biggest advantage of a variable rate. You can usually make unlimited extra repayments, pay down your loan as quickly as you like and use a full offset account to reduce the interest you pay. If you want to refinance, restructure your loan, or make changes like adding or removing a borrower, a variable rate makes the process far simpler because there are no break fees. This freedom is the main reason many first-home buyers choose variable rate loans. Life changes, and they want a loan that can change with them.

Of course, the downside is that your repayments aren't stable. If rates rise, your repayments will increase, sometimes more than once a year. You need to be comfortable with that movement in your budget, especially early on when finances can feel tight.

Variable rates tend to suit buyers who expect their income to grow; who plan to renovate or refinance in the near future; or who simply want the ability to adjust their loan without penalty. They're ideal for anyone who values flexibility over certainty: people who'd rather keep their options open than lock in a fixed rate for several years.

A variable loan is about freedom, while a fixed loan is about certainty. Neither is 'better': it just depends on your personality, your plans and how much movement your budget can comfortably handle.

Loan structures and types

Interest rates are only one part of the big picture when it comes to mortgages. Your *structure* can save — or cost — you tens of thousands of dollars.

Structure considerations include:

- whether you need an offset account
- whether part of the loan should be fixed
- whether you need the flexibility to redraw
- whether the property will become an investment later on
- how to structure the loan using a parental guarantee
- whether it's better to borrow the fees associated with loans or pay them upfront.

As a first-home buyer, you may not know yet whether your first home will eventually become an investment property. But your broker should always consider that possibility and structure the loan in a way that keeps your future options open. Good structure creates choice; bad structure locks you in.

Repayment types

There are generally two main repayment types: principal & interest, and interest only.

PRINCIPAL & INTEREST (P&I)

With a P&I loan, each repayment chips away at two things:

- the amount you originally borrowed (the principal)
- the cost of borrowing that money (the interest).

In the early years, the bulk of your repayment goes towards interest because your loan balance is at its highest (see figure 3.3). As time passes and the principal starts to fall, a larger portion of each repayment begins reducing the balance itself. This gradual shift is what helps you build equity in your home — slowly at first, then more noticeably as your loan progresses.

P&I loans are usually best for:

- first-home buyers living in the home
- long-term holding
- predictable equity growth.

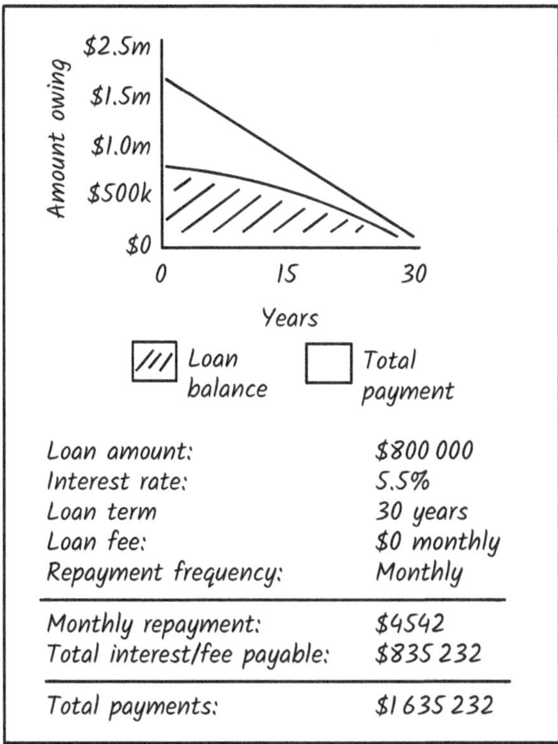

Figure 3.3: an example of a P&I loan

INTEREST-ONLY (IO)

With an IO loan, your repayments cover only the interest on the amount you've borrowed. This means that during the interest-only period, the principal does not reduce.

Interest-only loans are commonly used by investors, or borrowers who want to free up cash flow in the short term. They can also be part of a short-term strategy; for example, if you plan to refinance, sell or switch to P&I repayments later. While IO loans can make monthly payments lower, it's important to remember that the principal remains unchanged, so, while you are building equity in your property with the value increasing, you are not reducing the loan amount over time. See figure 3.4 (overleaf).

IO loans are usually best for investors looking to maximise cash flow.

Sherry bought an investment property and chose a variable interest-only loan so she could save for her future home. She placed the savings into her offset account, reducing interest charged and building her deposit for the next purchase.

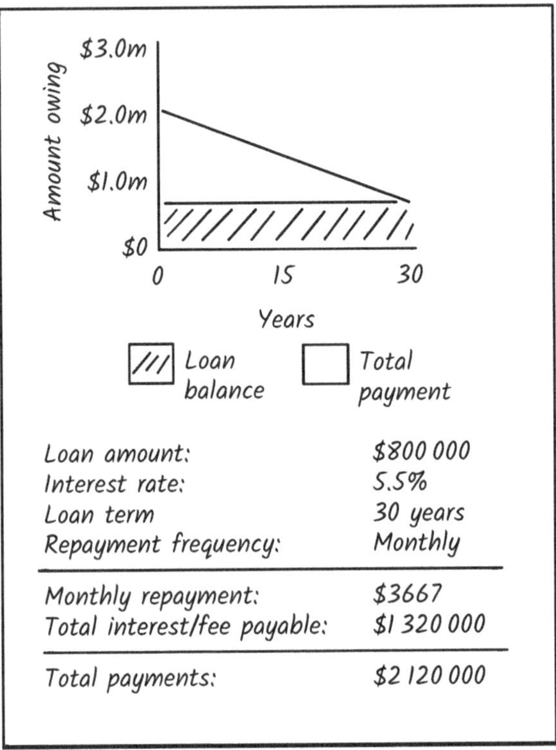

Figure 3.4: interest-only repayment breakdown over time

If you have a home loan and an investment loan, it often makes sense to direct extra repayments towards your home loan, not the investment loan, as the home-loan interest is not tax-deductible.

Offset accounts

An offset account is a bank account that you can link to your mortgage. Any savings or cash you add to this account is offset against your mortgage, reducing the amount of interest you pay. See the examples in figures 3.5 and 3.6.

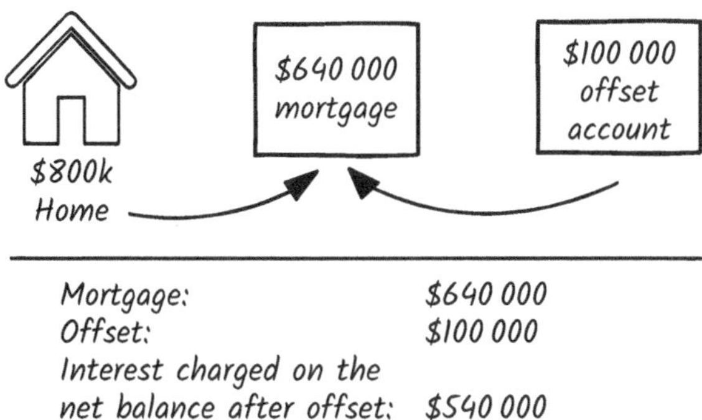

Figure 3.5: a single offset account

Figure 3.6: multiple offset accounts

Redraw

A redraw facility lets you take back any extra repayments you've made on your loan, essentially enabling you to access any money you've paid above the minimum required. It can act like a built-in safety buffer if you ever need those funds again. You can also choose to switch the redraw feature off if you think you might be tempted to dip into it. Just keep in mind that redraw facilities don't offer immediate access to cash, like offset accounts do.

Offset vs redraw

A fundamental difference between offset and redraw accounts is accessibility. Offset funds sit in a separate bank account from your loan and save you interest on your loan. This money is available to you at any time and the bank can't restrict your access to it. In contrast, the terms of a redraw account can depend on bank policy. Redraw funds sit inside your loan balance and are subject to the bank's terms and conditions, meaning that there may be processing times or delays when accessing redraw funds. Although rare, there have been cases where banks have frozen access to redraw accounts.

If you're buying an investment property, or your property will become an investment property in the future, offset is key. Money in your offset account is not paid off the loan so you have the flexibility to use those funds and the loan is still fully tax deductible. If, on the other hand, you had put that money in redraw, while the interest would still be zero, you would have technically paid the loan down so it can never be tax deductible again.

Most people reading this book, statistically speaking, will be buying a property to live in that will never be used as an investment property (they might invest, but not with this property). So, let's take a look at the difference between offset and redraw for owner-occupied home owners and how your mindset comes into this.

ACCESS TO MONEY CHANGES BEHAVIOUR

On paper, offset and redraw can both reduce the amount of interest you pay and your loan term. But in real life, they are experienced very differently.

Rach has clients to whom she would never recommend holding large sums of money in an offset account—not because offset is a bad product but because, for them, being able to easily access their money means they will use it.

Those same funds sitting in redraw? Completely safe. In fact, some of these clients deliberately make additional repayments to the loan and turn redraw access *off* to remove the temptation entirely.

These people know themselves well enough to say, 'If I can see it, I'll spend it'. And that self-awareness is powerful.

At the other end of the spectrum, Rach sees clients who are too restrictive. They are so focused on paying off their home loan quickly that they lock all their money into redraw and avoid touching it at all costs.

But then life happens and instead of using the redraw they put expenses on a credit card and don't pay their card off every month.

There's zero point in making extra contributions to a home loan at 5 or 6 per cent interest and simultaneously paying 18 per cent on credit card interest. This isn't discipline and it's counterproductive.

OFFSET WORKS BEST FOR 'BUCKET' PEOPLE

Some people are natural savers and like having money 'buckets' to save for things. If you're like this, multiple offset accounts are a game changer.

Think about how you saved your deposit (if you did):

- Did you separate your money into different accounts?
- Did you allocate funds for specific purposes?

If yes, multiple offsets may suit you very well.

Rach uses offset accounts as buckets. She has:

- an everyday account that her salary is credited to
- a bills account
- a school fees account
- a holiday account
- a future-investment account.

If her home-loan rate were currently 6 per cent, she would effectively be earning 6 per cent tax free on the combined balance of all those offset accounts, reducing the interest on her loan. That money isn't meant to pay off her loan. It's there to give her clarity, structure and flexibility.

Rach also uses redraw. For her, redraw represents money that she has paid into her loan above the required repayments. And psychologically, that money is 'done'. She doesn't plan to use it. She doesn't turn redraw off because she trusts herself not to use it. If she had a different mindset, she absolutely would turn it off.

Glen also teaches using multiple offset accounts as part of The Glen James Spending Plan.

To determine whether you're a saver or a spender, consider:

- your spending habits
- your triggers
- your relationship with access to cash.

Think about your relationship with money and talk to your mortgage broker about it before choosing the best loan set-up for you and your goals.

Loan term

Most home buyers choose a 30-year loan term but you can pay it off faster anytime and you can shorten the term later. If you're buying well below your means, you can set a lower loan term at the start. There's no rule that says it must be 30 years. Some lenders now offer 40-year loans! But the key takeaway is that these loan terms can be varied.

Construction loans

If you choose a house-and-land package or you buy land then build, chances are you're going to need a construction loan. The key difference with construction loans is that instead of receiving the full amount upfront, the bank releases funds in stages as your home reaches key milestones such as slab, frame, lock-up and completion.

While building, you generally only pay interest on the drawn funds, helping with cash flow. Once the build is finished, the loan converts to a standard P&I mortgage. These loans are also referred to as 'progressive draw-down loans' as they get larger the more they are drawn down. Construction loans can also be used for major renovations down the track.

First-home buyers can combine a construction loan with other schemes and grants—for example, the 5% Deposit Scheme—allowing for a purchase or build with just a 5 per cent deposit and no LMI. Most states also offer grants or concessions for new builds, including first-homeowner grants or stamp duty savings, although conditions vary by location. For example, in New South Wales, eligible first-home buyers building a new home can receive a grant of up to $10 000, which can be used towards the construction costs. By combining these options, first-home buyers can reduce upfront costs and make building more achievable.

Additional repayments

You can make additional repayments to most (variable and some fixed) loans whenever you like. The great part about additional repayments is that they are applied straight off the principal. Figures 3.7 and 3.8 demonstrate how additional repayments impact a typical mortgage with a loan amount of $500 000, based on contributing an extra $100/week and an extra $300/week respectively. Note how much shorter the loan term becomes with additional repayments! If you can avoid a $300/week car loan repayment and pay that towards your mortgage instead, there are big savings to enjoy.

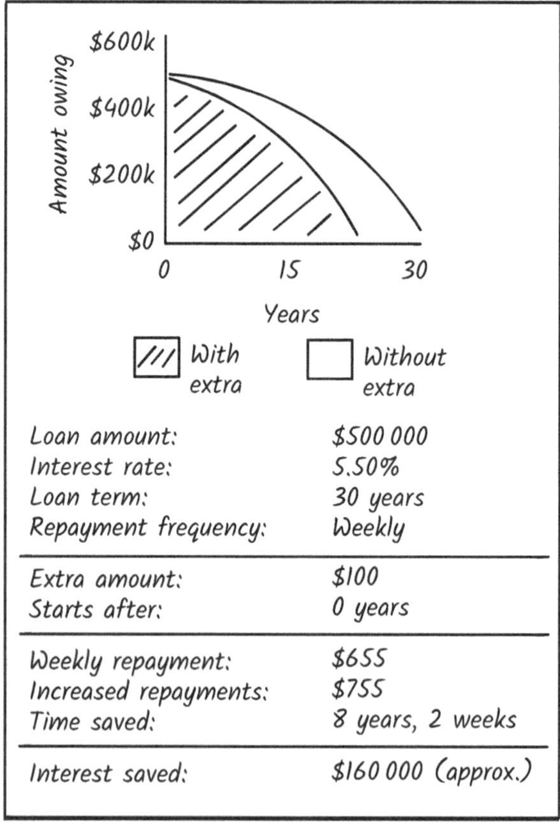

Figure 3.7: paying an extra $100/week

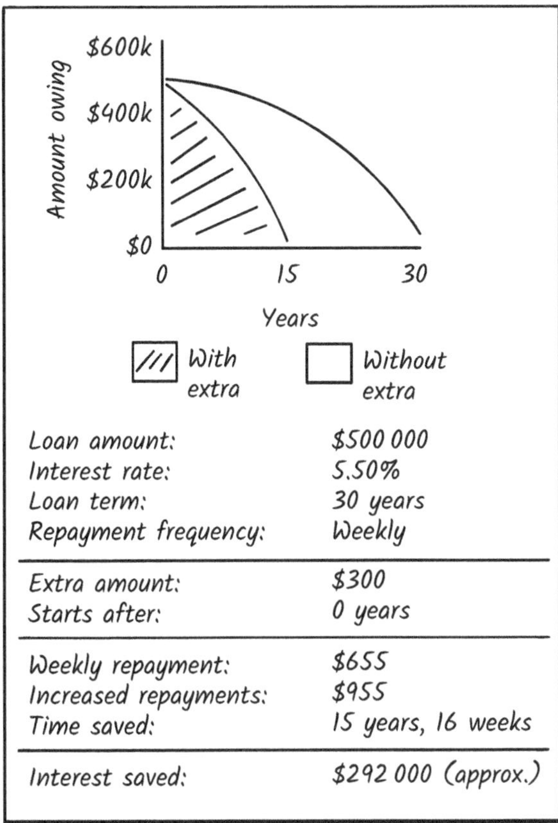

Figure 3.8: paying an extra $300/week

Equity

Equity, when referring to property, is the portion of your property that you truly own. It is worked out by assessing the current value of the property, then deducting the amount you owe.

'Usable equity' is how much of that amount you can actually keep or use. If you were to sell the property you would get all of it (minus selling costs). However, if you held that property and wanted to use the equity for, say, a home renovation or building wealth through other investments, there's a percentage rule for usable equity.

In most cases it's calculated at 80 per cent of the equity, but many professionals can go to 90 per cent. Some people may choose to pay LMI and access more. Figure 3.9 shows how this works.

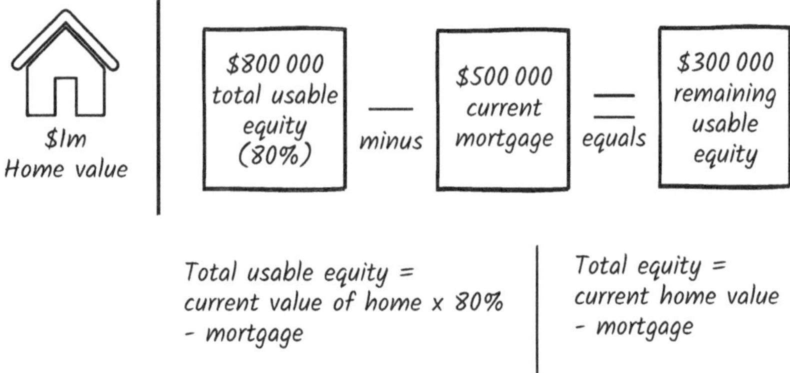

Figure 3.9: how usable equity works

> If your home is worth $700000 and you borrow $600000, you own about 85 per cent of it (that is, your LVR is 85 per cent). You actually own $100000 worth of your home, but you don't really have any usable equity because the bank will say you are at your maximum equity (because you owe more than 80 per cent of the value of your home).
>
> Let's fast-forward five years. Your property's value has increased to $900000 and you've paid down your loan by $70000. You now owe $530000. Your LVR is now 58 per cent and you own $370000 of your home. You also have $190000 in 'usable equity' because 80 per cent of $900000 is $720000, and $720000 minus your debt of $530000 is $190000.

> Equity can be used for investing in shares, investment properties and personal purposes such as renovations or even holidays, or just to negotiate your home lending rate. The bank would have given you a rate for 85 per cent LVR five years ago. But now they will sharpen their pencil for a 58 per cent LVR—they're facing much less risk and you're now statistically less likely to default on your mortgage.

As well as waiting for your home's value to increase so you have equity, you might also be waiting for a particular life event to arrive. Are you planning a family? Will you want to upsize your home? Before you use your equity for one purpose, think about whether you might need it later for another.

When you're looking at taking out equity, your mortgage broker will help by running the scenarios for you. If you have a goal that involves using equity, stay in touch with your broker as your equity amount grows and see how your situation changes every year. What would it look like if you bought an investment property? What would it look like repayment wise if you borrowed $50 000 for a renovation using your available equity?

It's important to understand how equity works and how it can be used to gain wealth. While it's exciting to pay off your home by the time you're in your 40s, it's worth knowing beforehand how you could use the equity in your home for other investments even while you're still paying it off. Take the opportunity to understand everything you can about the power of equity.

The point of all this

We've hit you with a lot in this chapter, right? At the end of the day, smart borrowing is less about chasing the 'perfect' product and more about understanding how different loan features shape your long-term position. Running detailed scenarios — with and without HELP debt, fixed vs variable rates, different repayment structures and the like — helps you see the real impact on your borrowing power and cash flow. Working closely with a mortgage broker can take a lot of the guesswork out of this, giving you personalised guidance and helping you set things up in a way that supports your goals. The clearer you are about what you want to achieve in the next few years, the easier it is to build a borrowing strategy that gives you confidence, flexibility and room to grow.

In chapter 4, we're going to introduce some quick-start hacks that may support your borrowing and help you get into the market in a creative (or even faster) way — so stick around.

Start with this . . .

Take some time to consider the following:

- * Are you ready to sit down with a mortgage broker and have an initial discussion?
- * What buying scenarios come to mind for you: buying a home first? Buying an investment first?
- * How much could you put in savings each time you're paid, to support your property buying?

4

Quick-start hacks to enter the market

For first-home buyers, it can feel like the goal posts are constantly moving: save more, earn more ...

But property buying has changed, and so have the associated strategies. The next generation of home owners are not doing things the way their parents did. They're rentvesting instead of settling in one spot; tapping into government schemes and incentives; and co-buying with friends or family, or even with the government in some cases. They're relying more than ever on family equity or funds and this, like it or hate it, is adding to the divide. Most are finding smarter, faster and more creative ways to get on the ladder, without waiting another five years to scrape together a 20 per cent deposit.

This chapter isn't about shortcuts. It's about practical options that first-home buyers are using right now to buy sooner, reduce costs and build wealth through property. Whether you're a first-home buyer looking for their first step on the property ladder, a couple looking for their dream home, a first-home buyer looking to invest or a first-home buyer who isn't sure what they want yet, but knows they want to get in, this chapter is for you.

> Top tip: use whatever is available to you and focus on entering the market. There's a lot you can't control, but you need to assess your situation and identify what you can leverage to your advantage. Aim to get as much wind in your sails as possible so that when you can enter the market, you launch off at a good pace.

National government grants and incentives

In Australia, there are state-based and federal schemes available to help people buy a home. These change over time, and the best way to stay up to date is by speaking with your mortgage broker.

You can't control what grants or incentives will be available when you're ready to buy. The goal is to get into the market and make the most of the government schemes available at the time. You shouldn't delay buying in the hope of qualifying for a future scheme, but you should absolutely use any incentives available that don't compromise your strategy. For many buyers, these schemes make the difference between owning a home or not.

We're going to have a look at what's available in 2026, including the latest updates. If you're on a savings plan, check in with your mortgage broker at key milestones to ensure nothing has changed.

> These incentives or grants can be layered or used in conjunction with one another. You might get a stamp duty concession as a state-based incentive and also use the Australian Government 5% Deposit Scheme. In addition, you could save a deposit using the First Home Super Saver (FHSS) scheme. If you're building or buying you might also be eligible for a state-based first-home buyers grant. Present everything to your mortgage broker and build whatever grant/scheme-layered cake you can!

The national schemes consist of these programs:

- First Home Super Saver (FHSS) scheme
- Australian Government 5% Deposit Scheme — low deposit and no LMI
- Australian Government Help to Buy Scheme — shared ownership with the government.

First Home Super Saver (FHSS) scheme

The FHSS scheme is a federal government initiative that allows first-home buyers to add voluntary contributions into their superannuation fund as a way to save faster towards a first-home deposit. It can only be used for a property that you will live in, not an investment property.

This scheme isn't used by many first-home buyers because either they don't know about it, or it's too complicated to understand.

It's a clever way to use your super account to save for your first home and it comes with some nice tax advantages. To use the scheme, you make extra contributions into your super fund on top of what your employer pays (that's your 12 per cent superannuation guarantee (SG) payment). When the time comes to buy your home, you can withdraw that extra money plus any earnings (a deemed amount set by the Australian Tax Office (ATO)) to put towards your first-home deposit. The reason there's a deemed amount is because if there were any share market downturns, you could effectively withdraw some of your retirement savings to put towards the deposit.

You may contribute up to $15 000 per year and a total of $50 000 over your lifetime under the scheme. These amounts sit within the broader pre-tax superannuation limit (concessional contribution) of $32 500 per year (which includes your employer's 12 per cent SG payment).

The big win is the tax rate: instead of paying your normal income tax, which could easily be over 30 per cent, these contributions (or first-home savings) are only taxed at 15 per cent.

This scheme is essentially a tax-saving play. You run money through super to fund some or all of your first-home deposit. There's an investment return component—likely better than your bank account interest rate—but the main advantage comes from the tax savings.

The overall tax savings under the FHSS scheme are approximately as follows:

* Income above $45 000 (tax rate of 32 per cent): tax saving of ~$7650
* Income above $135 000 (tax rate of 39 per cent): tax saving of ~$8175

- Income above \$190 000 (tax rate of 47 per cent): tax saving of ~\$8775
- Income above \$250 000 (tax rate of 47 per cent but 30 per cent contribution tax): tax saving of ~\$2550

Note that:

- these tax rates include the 2 per cent Medicare levy
- the overall tax savings include income tax and superannuation contribution tax
- this strategy has no real benefit if you earn under \$45 000.

Let's compare this to how most people save for a house. Usually, you get paid, tax comes out and whatever's left lands in your bank account. You might move some of that money into a savings account or invest it, but it's all after-tax money.

Figure 4.1 (overleaf) demonstrates how normal savings works, without adding any of your own money into super.

PAYING MONEY INTO SUPER FOR THE FHSS SCHEME

There are two ways to get money into super if you want to use the FHSS scheme, and both end up in the same place. The difference is how and when the tax benefit shows up. It's important to note, this is no different from how you would add money to your super fund in a tax-effective manner if you weren't planning to use the scheme. You don't need to tell your employer or super fund that the additional pre-tax contributions are for the FHSS scheme.

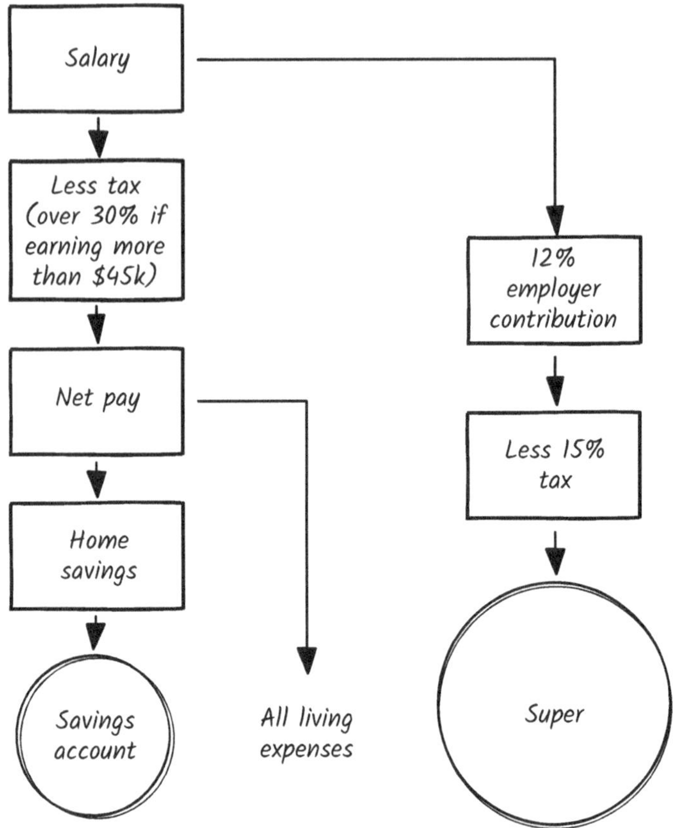

Figure 4.1: normal home savings

- *Option 1: salary sacrifice through your employer*
  Figure 4.2 illustrates how salary sacrificing works to contribute to superannuation as a concessional contribution (in this instance you are doing it for the purpose of using the FHSS scheme, and the amount needs to remain under the scheme's annual cap of $15 000).
  When you ask your employer to direct part of your pay into your super fund on top of the compulsory 12 per cent SG, the ATO can see that these are additional contributions, not employer contributions. Anything above your 12 per cent employer contribution is called a 'reportable superannuation

contribution'. Because the money goes straight into super before you're paid, your take-home pay is lower.

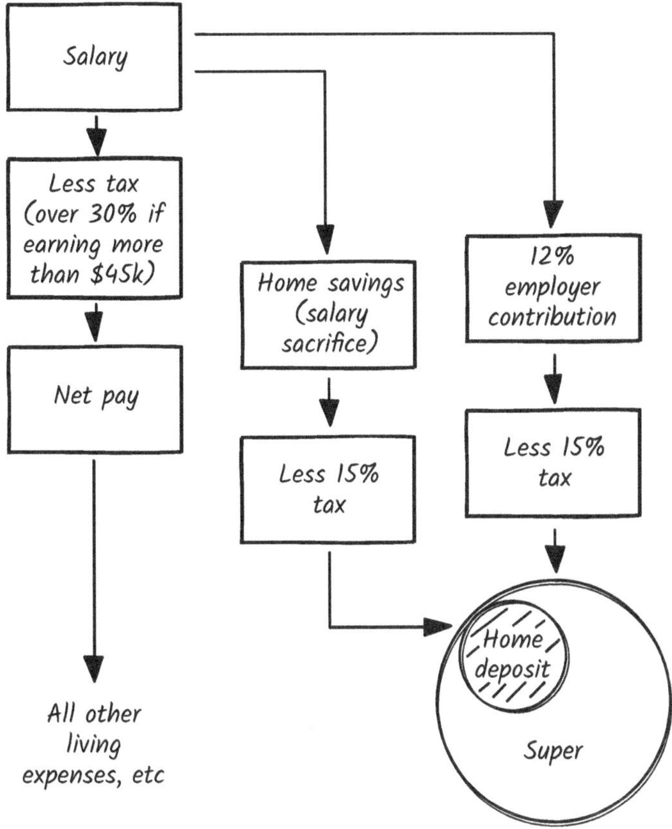

Figure 4.2: salary sacrificing through your employer

- *Option 2: make personal contributions*
  Figure 4.3 (overleaf) shows how you contribute money from your savings into super as a personal deductible contribution. You pay the money into your super fund, where it is treated similarly to a salary sacrifice contribution. You must notify your super fund that you intend to claim a tax deduction by lodging a Notice of Intent. The fund then applies the 15 per cent contributions tax, and you claim the deduction in your personal tax return.

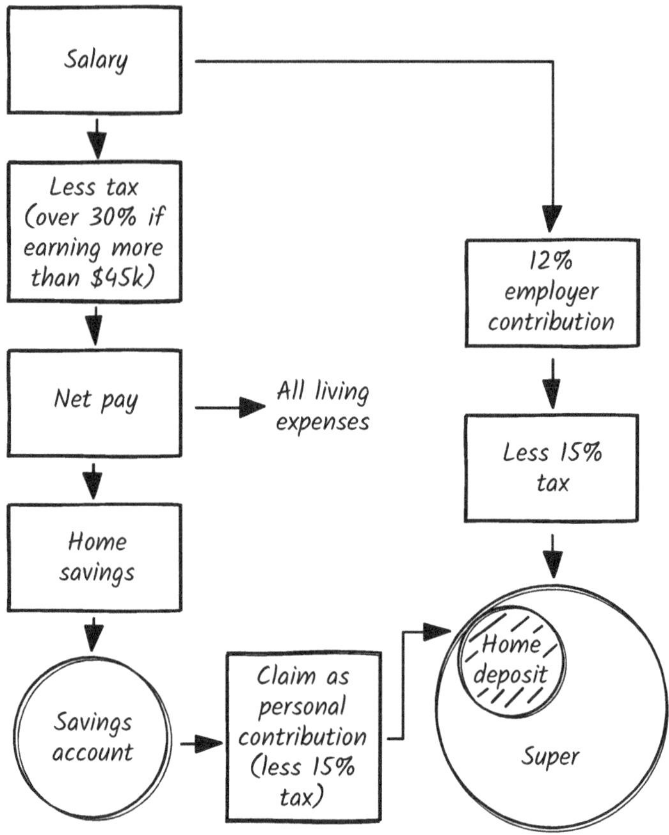

Figure 4.3: making personal deductible contributions

You continue receiving your normal pay, save money in your own bank account and contribute it to super whenever you choose. This can be done as a lump sum or through regular contributions during the year. Lodging the Notice of Intent ensures the contribution is treated as tax deductible.

This approach can be useful if you have a HELP debt. Salary sacrifice reduces the tax withheld during the year, which may increase your HELP repayment at tax time. Making personal deductible contributions instead can help smooth the end of year tax outcome.

The key admin rule is simple. You must lodge the Notice of Intent to Claim with your super fund after you stop contributing for that financial year and before you lodge your tax return. If you accidentally contributed $16 000 in a year, you would tell your super fund, on the Notice of Intent to Claim form, to only allocate $15 000 as a personal deductible contribution.

If your employer contributions are already at or near the $32 500 concessional contribution cap, you might not have as much room to use this scheme, unless you've got unused 'carry-forward' contributions from previous years.

USING SUPER MONEY FOR YOUR FIRST HOME

When you're finally ready to buy your first home, you'll apply to the ATO and they will give you a determination that your fund will need to release your FHSS scheme savings and earnings.

The money comes out at your marginal tax rate, but you get a 30 per cent tax credit. And just like that, your tax-smart savings strategy turns into part of your home deposit.

> Another major win in using the FHSS scheme is that you can't spend the money you're saving. If you're like Glen and you're a spender, it can be tempting to spend your deposit before you need it on that new thing you really need (*note:* you don't really need it). Locking the cash away in your super fund also comes with the added benefit of 'out of sight, out of mind'—and out of your hands.

MORE ON THE FHSS SCHEME

There are a few final rules and realities worth reiterating. You can contribute up to $15 000 per financial year under the scheme, on top of your employer contributions. However, you still need to stay within the $32 500 per year concessional cap, which includes your 12 per cent employer contributions and any salary sacrifice or deductible personal contributions. The lifetime limit for FHSS withdrawals is $50 000.

Within those limits, this is one of the smartest and least-used ways to boost a first-home deposit, all inside the tax-friendly world of super.

If you decide not to go ahead and use the FHSS scheme, you're not trapped. There are ways to get the money back out of super, although a penalty will apply. This isn't the end of the world, so don't stress. You also might already have money sitting there without realising it, if you have salary sacrificed since the scheme started on 1 July 2017. Those contributions may already count and could be used towards your deposit, provided they sit under the annual caps.

For those who really want to nerd out, there is an advanced option. You can set up a second super fund with no insurance attached and a more conservative investment option, then manually contribute to that fund from your bank account and lodge a Notice of Intent to Claim each year in which you claim that amount on your tax. That way, this fund becomes a dedicated first-home savings bucket, separate from your long-term retirement money. This matters because the scheme uses a deemed rate set by the ATO, and market movements can affect outcomes. Keeping it separate helps you mentally and practically quarantine this strategy from your future retirement savings. Just remember, the FHSS and general super caps apply across all your super accounts. Having multiple funds doesn't give you extra room.

If any of this feels unclear, pick up the phone and call your super fund. You pay member fees and they provide help. Ask them how they support members using the scheme.

This is not a loophole or a gimmick. It's a genuine tax-saving strategy. It's effectively free money. It is confusing, which is exactly why so many people give it a miss.

One final and very practical point. If you're buying at auction, make sure you apply for your ATO determination before auction day. As part of the process, you must declare that you have not previously purchased a property. If you win at auction and then apply, you've technically already bought a home and that can derail the whole thing. Timing matters.

If you're not already using the scheme and your employer contribution is not more than $17 500, you have cash saved in your bank account (say $30 000), and you plan to buy in the short term, here's what you could do to move that money through the FHSS and access the tax benefits:

* In June, put $15 000 into your super from your bank account, submit a Notice of Intent to Claim and claim it as a personal contribution on your tax return for the current financial year.
* In July, put $15 000 into your super from your bank account, and submit a notice of Intent to Claim.
* Contact the ATO, obtain a ruling and then release the funds.
* Claim the second $15 000 contribution on your tax return next financial year.

Now, the above will work provided your timing is over two financial years. You don't need to use the full $50 000 amount that the scheme allows, nor do you have to contribute $15 000 per year. As we have seen, the maximum tax savings relate to using the full $50 000 over a number of financial years. However, any amount you use via this scheme will help you save tax.

If you have a spouse or partner, you can use the scheme together. Your mortgage broker can help coordinate the timing and paperwork, and once you understand the steps, the process is actually quite straightforward. Slightly fiddly at first, but worth it.

Australian Government 5% Deposit Scheme

This scheme offers a low deposit and no LMI:

- Minimum 5 per cent deposit for first-home buyers
- Minimum 2 per cent deposit for single parents.

WHAT THE SCHEME INVOLVES

The Australian Government 5% Deposit Scheme is a national initiative designed to help eligible buyers purchase a home with a low deposit and no LMI. It works like a parental guarantee, except the guarantor is the government.

Buyers can enter the market with only a 5 per cent deposit (or 2 per cent for eligible single parents), avoiding the tens of thousands of dollars usually charged in LMI fees when borrowing more than 80 per cent.

The scheme was originally for first-home buyers only, but it has since expanded to include anyone who hasn't owned property in the previous 10 years. However, state-based stamp duty concessions only apply to first-home buyers at the time of writing.

Check the federal government website (www.firsthomebuyers.gov.au) to see the current property price caps for this scheme in your region, state or territory.

KEY RULE

The main restriction is that the property must remain owner-occupied for as long as the scheme is in place. There is no fixed time period: the guarantee ends when your LVR reaches 80 per cent (either through property value growth, paying down the loan or both). Until then, you can't convert the home into an investment property unless you refinance out of the scheme, potentially with LMI. For long-term owner-occupiers, this isn't an issue, but for buyers planning future renting, relocating or rentvesting, it's important to understand.

Joe's and Tiarne's incomes: $95 000 and $98 000 respectively

Savings: $40 000

Target property: $700 000 townhouse

Costs and loan structure:

* Purchase price + costs: $705 000
* Deposit: $40 000
* Loan: $665 000
* Approx. repayments at 5.5 per cent: $3800 per month
* Stamp duty: $0 (FHB concession)
* LMI saved: approx. $26 000

By using the 5% Deposit Scheme, Joe and Tiarne avoided LMI and entered the market much sooner.

Australian Government Help to Buy Scheme

This scheme gives you shared ownership with the government:

- Minimum 2 per cent deposit
- 10 000 spots available.

WHAT THE SCHEME INVOLVES

The Help to Buy scheme is a shared equity program. Unlike the 5% Deposit Scheme, where the government acts as a guarantor, here the government buys a share of the property. You only need a 2 per cent deposit and the government's share reduces the size of your loan.

You don't pay rent on the government's share, but the government owns a percentage of your home (typically 30 to 40 per cent) and any increase in the property's value applies to their share. The scheme is intended to make home ownership possible for people who may otherwise struggle to enter the market.

KEY RULES

This scheme has a few rules:

- Property must be owner-occupied for the duration of the scheme
- You can't already own property in Australia or overseas (exceptions for single parents buying out an ex-partner)
- Income caps: $100 000 for singles, $160 000 for couples and single parents
- State and regional price caps apply
- Must be an Australian citizen (if buying as a couple, both must be)
- Not all lenders offer this; criteria and pricing vary.

EXITING THE SCHEME

The Help to Buy scheme is not a lifelong commitment. Once you're in your home, you can exit by:

- making incremental payments to increase your equity
- refinancing to buy out the government's share when your borrowing capacity allows
- selling the property.

Important: As your property value rises, the government's share value also increases. When you buy them out or sell, you pay their current share value, not the original contribution.

Here's a practical, simplified example:

- You want to buy a $500 000 home
- Deposit: $10 000 (2 per cent)
- Government share: $150 000 (30 per cent)
- Loan amount: $340 000
- You manage all ongoing costs (loan, rates, insurance)
- Owner-occupied rules apply until you buy out the government's share.

This scheme is especially useful for buyers who have no other options available to them. It enables them to buy where they want to live, though it's less flexible if you want to relocate or rent out the property at some stage.

A word of caution

On the surface, these national, first-home buyer schemes can look very attractive. They reduce the deposit required and remove the need for LMI, which is understandably appealing for buyers struggling to save a full deposit.

However, there are aspects of these schemes that first-home buyers need to understand very clearly before committing.

HOW THESE SCHEMES DIFFER FROM STATE-BASED ASSISTANCE

Traditional state-based incentives such as stamp duty concessions or the First Home Owner Grant typically come with a clear and limited requirement: you must live in the property for a defined period, often 6 or 12 months. After that, you're generally free to make decisions that suit your circumstances. The national schemes are different. They introduce ongoing obligations that don't always have a clear end date.

KEY RESTRICTIONS TO UNDERSTAND

Two conditions of these national schemes in particular raise concerns for us:

1. *You must live in the property for an undefined period.*
   You're required to live in the property until you're able to refinance and remove the government's involvement. This time frame is unascertainable. It might be one year. It could just as easily be five. Until that point, you generally can't lease out the property. This removes a strategy that many first-home buyers rely on when circumstances change.
2. *There are limits on how much cash you're allowed to retain.*
   There are restrictions on how much of your savings you

can keep out of the transaction. In practical terms, this often means:

- smaller cash buffers
- less flexibility
- reduced emergency reserves.

For buyers already stretching to enter the market, this can be risky.

> We love to promote buffers and emergency funds when buying your first home. When using certain government help, such as the 5% Deposit Scheme and the Help to Buy scheme, there are limits to how much of your buffer (or emergency fund cash) you can keep for yourself.
>
> The amount varies among lenders; however, it's generally around six months of living expenses. Since these new and updated schemes have been released Rach have seen clients put funds into the scheme that they would have preferred to leave out as a buffer or in an emergency account. It's worth making a plan with your broker well before you buy for how you'll handle this. Rach has seen people pivot and change from a government guarantee to a parental guarantee, or even to paying LMI, to avoid having these restrictions imposed.

WHY THIS MATTERS IN REAL LIFE

Most first-home buyers don't plan to run into trouble, but trouble rarely announces itself in advance.

When home owners experience job loss, illness or repayment stress, the most common strategy we see is:

- moving back in with parents or into cheaper accommodation
- renting out their home temporarily
- regaining stability before making long-term decisions.

This strategy is incredibly common and incredibly effective. However, under these national schemes, this option may not be available.

When you combine the inability to rent out the property if things get tough with a reduced cash buffer, you increase the risk of being forced to sell—potentially in a market that doesn't suit you. And forced sales rarely produce good outcomes.

WHY FLEXIBILITY MATTERS MORE THAN ENTRY SPEED

These schemes aren't inherently bad. For buyers with very stable circumstances, they may be appropriate. But first-home buying is rarely static. Careers change. Relationships change. Health and family needs change. Flexibility is often more valuable than getting into the market slightly sooner. For this reason, we encourage buyers to consider all available options—not just the ones that appear cheapest upfront.

This may include:

- paying LMI
- using a parental guarantee
- buying at a lower price point with stronger buffers.

Sometimes the 'more expensive' option on paper is the safer one in practice.

Government schemes are designed to help, but they aren't one-size-fits-all solutions. By the time you buy, the rules may have changed, but regardless of what they are when you buy, consider all of the options and ask a mortgage broker to break down the fine print about the scheme. Before committing, you need to understand not just how a scheme helps you buy, but how it may restrict you after you've bought. The right decision isn't the one that gets you into a property fastest. It's the one that still works if life doesn't go exactly to plan.

State-based incentives

The main state-based incentives are stamp duty waivers, which reduce the major upfront cost of stamp / transfer duty; and first-home buyer grants, which usually provide a cash bonus when you build or buy a new home. As we've mentioned, state-based incentives change regularly, but here's a high-level summary.

Stamp / transfer duty concessions

One of the biggest costs in buying a home is tax. Every time you buy a property, you pay a tax known as stamp duty (also called transfer duty). Stamp duty is paid to your state or territory authority for the right to transfer ownership of a property from one person to another. You may be exempt from paying stamp duty in your state if you're a first-home buyer, depending on the purchase price.

At the time of writing, if you were buying for $800 000, the following stamp duty would be payable:

- *ACT:* $22 158, but $0 for first-home buyers who earn less than $250 000
- *NSW:* $30 412, but $0 for first-home buyers
- *NT:* $39 600 — same for first-home buyers, but you may get a $10 000 grant

- *Qld:* $21 850 — same for first-home buyers (if buying a property at $700 000, it would be $0)
- *SA:* $37 850 — same for first-home buyers. (However, if you buy land and build or buy a newly built home or apartment there is no stamp duty, and recently no price cap.)
- *Tas.:* $31 185 — same for first-home buyers (if buying a property at $700 000, it would be $0)
- *Vic.:* $43 070 — same for first-home buyers (if buying a property at $600 000, it would be $0)
- *WA:* $32 315 — same for first-home buyers (if buying a property at $500 000, it would be $0).

The timing of paying stamp duty costs also depends on your state or territory, but generally expect it to be paid around the time of settlement. You'll need to confirm this with your state or territory revenue office.

First-home-buyer grants

At the time of writing, as state governments are trying to encourage the building of new homes, first-home-buyer grants are attached to new homes only. This includes buying land and building, buying a house-and-land package, buying a home that someone else built but has never lived in, and sometimes a substantially renovated home is included. Table 4.1 lists the grant amounts and conditions related to state-based home-buying schemes as at 2026.

These amounts and conditions change frequently. Meet with your mortgage broker to find out what opportunities you can take advantage of to boost your chances of entering the market sooner rather than later.

Table 4.1: grant amounts and conditions related to state-based home-buying schemes by state / territory — 2026

State / Territory	Grant amount	Key conditions / Notes
New South Wales (NSW)	$10 000	For new homes. Eligible for homes up to a certain value (e.g. up to $600 000 for a build only, or up to $750 000 when combining land and build).
Victoria (Vic.)	$10 000	For new homes valued up to $750 000.
Queensland (Qld)	$30 000 (for certain contracts)	As of 20 Nov 2023 to 30 June 2025: $30 000 for eligible new homes valued at ≤ $750 000.
South Australia (SA)	$15 000	For eligible new homes.
Western Australia (WA)	$10 000	For new or substantially renovated homes. Property value caps depend on location (metro / regional).
Tasmania (Tas.)	$10 000 (current)	As of 1 July 2024 the FHOG is $10 000 for new homes. *Note:* Between 1 April 2021 and 30 June 2024, the grant was $30 000.
Northern Territory (NT)	$50 000 (new) / $10 000 (existing)	For new homes: up to $50 000 (HomeGrown Territory Grant). For established homes: $10 000 for first-home buyers.
Australian Capital Territory (ACT)	No FHOG	The FHOG has been replaced by other assistance (e.g. stamp duty concessions) in the ACT.

Property in action

Do some research on your state or territory revenue office website to learn about the state-specific grants or schemes available to first-home buyers at the time you're planning to buy.

Other ways to enter the market

Let's talk about the many creative ways we see first property buyers enter the market. These options improve your borrowing, give you more options and with some upfront planning they can help you get your foot in the door sooner.

Buying with family or friends

With people staying single longer and housing affordability tightening, more buyers are looking at purchasing property with a friend, sibling or family member. In many areas, singles are finding it harder to buy alone so buying with someone you trust can make home ownership achievable sooner. Even the government has recognised this shift, opening incentives like the Australian Government 5% Deposit Scheme to people who are not in a romantic relationship.

These arrangements can work beautifully and benefit everyone involved because they have benefits such as:

- a bigger combined deposit
- a borrowing capacity similar to that of a couple

- faster entry into the market (you can now layer all the same schemes and incentives available to couples)
- access to better locations and potentially a better asset
- shared ongoing costs.

But before you jump in, there are some important things to consider. Buying with someone, romantic partner or not, is a large commitment. Even if you separate your loans, in most cases you are still jointly liable for the entire debt. It's essential to talk openly about how you'll manage things while you own the property and what happens if life changes. Conversations may include:

- What happens if one wants to sell and the other doesn't?
- If one moves out, does the other pay rent for their share?
- How are expenses divided?
- What happens if someone's partner moves in?
- What happens if one person enters financial hardship?
- What is the long-term plan?
- If one wants to sell later (to buy with a romantic partner, for example) and that leaves the other unable to buy again, how will this be resolved?

Having these conversations upfront helps ensure everyone is on the same page before entering such a significant commitment. Life changes — partners, job relocations, kids — so a written agreement, or even a legal agreement, may be appropriate.

Troy and Jed, two brothers, bought a home together in 2023 using the Australian Government 5% Deposit Scheme. They separated their lending into two $300 000 loans. Although jointly liable for the full $600 000, separating the loans made their accounting easier. Troy made a lot of additional repayments; Jed paid the minimum.

By 2025, substantial equity had built up. Jed's loan was $280 000; Troy's was $220 000. Together they owed $500 000 and the property was worth $780 000. Troy had since partnered and wanted to buy a home with his partner. Jed was happy living in the property and didn't want to sell. Troy couldn't borrow enough for his next home unless the property was sold. Jed wasn't in a position to buy Troy out. They had never discussed what would happen if one wanted to sell and the other didn't.

The property ended up being sold:

- $780 000 sale price
- $23 800 sale costs
- $756 200 proceeds
- $500 000 mortgage payout
- *$256 200 net proceeds.*

Split based on their loan balances:

- Troy: $158 100
- Jed: $98 100.

There was no dispute over the split, but there was a major fallout over timing. Jed didn't want to sell. He had no partner, had used his one chance at the 5% Deposit Scheme and $98 100 wasn't enough for him to get back into the market. He had believed the property was a long-term hold; Troy had believed it was long-term until one of them met a partner. They were both 'right', but their expectations were different. A simple conversation before buying could have prevented the dispute or helped them agree on a minimum time frame or exit plan.

Joint ownership with parents or adult children

For many families facing soaring housing costs, another question is emerging: should we buy property together? Whether it's helping a child into their first home, wanting to keep the family close or making the numbers work in an expensive market, joint ownership between parents and adult children is becoming more common. But it carries lifelong financial and relationship implications and must be approached with clarity, structure and a plan.

Joint ownership is typically considered when income is needed to support the child's loan application, meaning a gift or parental guarantee won't be enough and the parent must own a share of the property. Families choose this path for reasons such as:

- helping someone afford the property they need
- keeping wealth in the family
- long-term intergenerational planning
- dual-occupancy living (e.g. a property with two homes or a granny flat).

Our view is not to do it if there's another option available. However, we've also seen it work extremely well when everyone's goals align and expectations are clear.

Dean and Macey wanted to buy acreage as Macey has horses. Their borrowing capacity capped them at around $800 000, but the suitable acreage properties were around $1 200 000.

Macey's mum, Carol, owned her home outright and wanted Dean and Macey close to her as she aged. Her home was worth $900 000. When a $1 500 000 property with two houses came up, they agreed to buy it together.

How it happened:

- Carol sold her home.
- All three purchased the $1 500 000 property as tenants in common:
    - Carol owned 50 per cent
    - Dean and Macey owned 50 per cent.

Financially:

- Dean and Macey's 50 per cent was worth $750 000, which they borrowed.
- Carol contributed $750 000 cash from her sale and banked the remainder.
- Carol was a guarantor (as an owner) but not responsible for repayments.

Legally:

- A solicitor prepared a comprehensive co-ownership agreement covering:
    - ownership shares
    - contributions
    - what happens if someone wants to exit
    - what happens if someone dies
    - dispute resolution.

Protecting the inheritance of Carol's other children meant Dean and Macey would need to pay out the siblings or the property would be sold. This was a unique situation that fit everyone's goals and shows how family co-ownership can be structured effectively.

The right way to buy with friends or family

To buy successfully with friends or family, ensure you do the following:

- *Choose the right ownership structure.* Joint tenants means equal ownership; tenants in common allows for different percentages (the next section goes into detail about these ownership structures). Most friends or siblings choose tenants in common for flexibility and protection.
- *Have the 'what if' conversations early.* Talk through all possible scenarios before signing anything.

- *Speak to a solicitor.* Understand the risks and what protections can be put in place.
- *Treat it like a business deal.* Get it all in writing: how expenses are split, how equity is divided, what happens on sale and how contributions are recognised.

Ownership structures and title

When you're buying in with others it's important to take a minute to touch on ownership structures and titles. When you buy a property, you sign a contract, money changes hands and your name goes on the title. Simple in theory. Underneath that, there are different ways ownership can be structured and those choices can have big implications for tax, estate planning and what happens if someone dies or relationships change. This section applies to both owner-occupied homes and investment properties and the information forms part of your overall strategy.

Sole ownership

Sole ownership is the simplest structure. One person owns 100 per cent of the property. Their name is on the title and they alone are responsible for the loan (even if someone else informally helps with repayments). This can make sense if you are single, if you are buying with a partner but for specific legal reasons only one of you should be on the title, or where one person is taking on the bulk of the financial risk. The flip side is that all the risk and liability sits with that one owner.

Joint tenants

Joint tenancy is very common for couples. Under a joint tenancy structure, two (or more) people own the property together. If one person dies, their share automatically passes to the surviving owner, regardless of what their will says. This is known as 'the right of survivorship'. Joint tenants are often assumed to own 50 per cent each, but the key feature is not the percentage, it's the automatic transfer on death. For many long-term couples, this is exactly what they want.

Tenants in common

Tenants in common is a different type of shared ownership where each owner holds a defined share and that share forms part of their estate when they die. For example, two people might own a property as tenants in common, with a 60 per cent and a 40 per cent split. If the 40 per cent owner dies, their share doesn't automatically pass to the other owner. Instead, it is dealt with under their will or under the laws of intestacy (that's if there's no will). Tenants in common can be useful where:

- friends, siblings or business partners are buying together
- there's a blended family situation and each person wants their share to ultimately pass to children from a previous relationship
- there's a deliberate tax or estate-planning strategy in place.

In some cases, there may also be arrangements such as life tenancy clauses, where a surviving partner is allowed to live in the property for life or for a certain period, after which the property must be sold and proceeds distributed to beneficiaries. This is why it's important to involve a lawyer or estate-planning specialist if your relationships or family structures are complex.

Company or trust ownership

Some properties are owned through a company or trust structure. This is more common for experienced investors or for people with specific asset-protection or tax-planning needs. For most first-home buyers and first-time investors, buying through a company or trust isn't necessary and can actually complicate borrowing. In recent years, many lenders have tightened their policies around company and trust borrowing. Building your strategy purely around a niche lending policy is risky, because those policies can change.

If you're considering a company or trust structure for genuine reasons, such as asset protection for a particular profession or multi-generational planning, that conversation belongs with your accountant and your lawyer. It should not be used as a shortcut just to squeeze a bit more borrowing capacity out of the system (as there can be different rules for borrowing in entities — although, slowly, some lenders are ceasing this altogether).

The main point is this: talk to your conveyancer, accountant and, if needed, an estate-planning lawyer about ownership structures before you start signing contracts. How you own the property is part of your overall strategy. It's much easier to choose the right structure upfront than to try to retrofit it later.

Family help

No doubt you've heard and read news stories about the increase in family members assisting first-home buyers to get into the market. The old bank of Mum and Dad! It's not an option for everyone, but it is an option for some, so let's talk about it. Whether it's a gift, a guarantee or rent-free accommodation while you save, it's great to know what's possible and how others have used this strategy to get ahead.

We'll explore different ways parents or families help people into home ownership and hopefully it will help open some doors to conversations about how these could work in your situation.

Rent-free accommodation while you save

Also known as the 'deposit accelerator', moving back in with family can be really hard after having been independent, but it can be the gateway to home ownership. We've already looked in depth at how the deposit is the biggest hurdle for first-home buyers, and with the cost of living being so high, it can seem impossible to save while renting.

If you're going to ask your family to support you in saving a deposit and sacrifice your own lifestyle, make sure you set a clear plan with a measurable goal and time frame so you don't waste this opportunity. Create a strict saving structure and have a determined amount direct debited into your savings account each pay cycle. A great tip is to base your savings target on what your mortgage payment and ongoing home ownership costs will be—you'll also get the added benefit of stress-testing your future mortgaged self. Know exactly how many weeks it will take to reach your goal and keep a visual reminder of what you're achieving and why.

Parental guarantees

A parental guarantee, also known as a family pledge or guarantor loan, allows parents to help their child buy a property by using equity in their own home or investment property as additional security. Instead of gifting cash for a deposit, the parents provide a limited guarantee that fills the security gap. This can allow the buyer to borrow up to 100 per cent of the purchase price (plus all costs such as stamp duty, buyers agent and legal fees), provided their income supports the repayments.

From the bank's perspective, two boxes still need to be ticked. First, the borrower must be able to service the full loan. Second, there must be enough total equity across the two properties to reduce the lender's risk.

Parental guarantees are commonly used by first-home buyers who can afford repayments but are stuck trying to save a deposit while renting. Parents don't usually need to contribute cash or make loan repayments. They simply provide security. Some lenders will accept guarantees from retired parents or even siblings. Choosing the right lender is about balancing what works best for your loan structure and what feels most comfortable for your parents in terms of risk and flexibility. In some cases, you and your parents may even end up with different lenders, which is where an experienced broker is essential.

LIMITED VS FULL GUARANTEES

There are two main types of guarantee: limited and full.

A limited guarantee caps the parents' exposure at a specific amount; for example, $200 000 on a $1 000 000 purchase.

A full guarantee places the parents' entire property on the line. Full guarantees carry significantly more risk and are now rare. In practice, limited guarantees are the safer and far more common option.

The goal is always to remove the guarantee as soon as possible once you've built enough equity or paid down enough debt for the property to stand on its own. Generally, equity growth can beat the loan reduction in the race to have the guarantee released.

You can see in figure 4.4 that:

- no cash contribution is required from the guarantor
- the guarantor does not need to service the loan
- parents can have an existing mortgage and still act as guarantors.

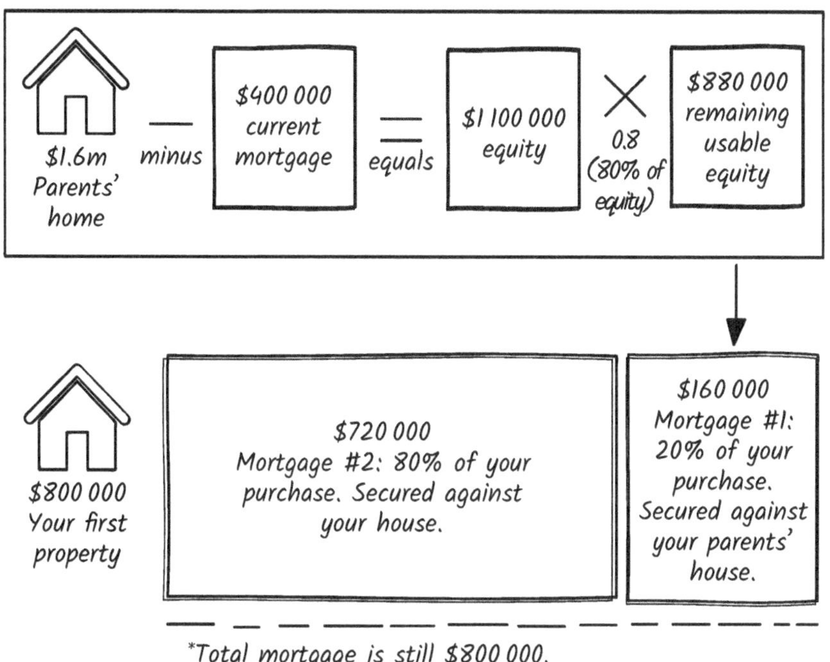

Figure 4.4: Family Guarantee security

Guarantees can often be released once the property value increases or the loan is paid down. Some lenders will allow parents to support more than one child at a time, subject to equity and valuations. Lender policies vary widely, so flexibility matters.

HOW THE STRUCTURE WORKS IN PRACTICE

While figure 4.4 shows two separate loans, in reality it may be a single loan with a limited security guarantee sitting in the background. In some cases, brokers can structure the guaranteed portion separately to help borrowers focus on paying that part down first (as a visual aid). The larger the buyer's cash deposit, the smaller the guarantee required.

Stamp duty and other purchase costs aren't shown in figure 4.4, but in some cases these costs can also be secured as part of the guaranteed portion, provided there is sufficient equity.

ARE PARENTS TAKING ON RISK?

Yes. The parents' property is being used as security for the guaranteed amount. Even with a limited guarantee, that amount is still tied to their home. If the loan defaults and the property is sold at a loss, the bank can pursue the guarantors up to the amount of the limited guarantee *or* the amount owed to the bank after the sale of the property, whichever is lower (though it can't exceed the guarantee amount).

This is why guarantees should always be limited, clearly understood and paired with a clear exit strategy. In some cases, parents can also downsize or move properties and the guarantee moved to the new property.

Before using a parental guarantee, check for the following:

- Emergency buffers should already be in place.
- A guarantee is not a substitute for good saving habits; it simply shortens the waiting time.
- Avoid guarantees if you — the borrower — have unstable income, high personal debt or no savings discipline.
- Strong financial foundations matter: a solid spending plan, appropriate insurances, and wills and estate planning should be in place.

In practice, this is a low-risk strategy for those who have parents with equity in their home and both you and your parents are fully aware of how the arrangement is set up.

Gifting

Australia is in the middle of the largest intergenerational wealth transfer in history. According to the Commonwealth Bank, over the next two decades, baby boomers are expected to pass on more than one trillion dollars in property, superannuation and investments to their children. Much of this is already happening—not just through inheritance, but also through living gifts to help the next generation buy property.

Gifting is an extremely popular way for parents to help family members into the property market, especially when parents might be a bit cautious about a parental guarantee. Here are some high-level considerations if that's you or your parents' situation:

- *Gifts:* These are generally smaller amounts; no hold on property; most lenders will take gifts as genuine savings.
- *Parental guarantees:* No cash needed; parents can keep their money invested; security only.

> Some lenders even include gifts as 'genuine savings', so the gift doesn't need to be held for a certain amount of time before buying.

Sometimes the gift is just the minimum deposit needed, as the deposit is the main hurdle. Other times, the gift is used to reduce the loan amount because only a certain loan size can be obtained.

If a parent is considering gifting a property, it's worth noting that this may trigger capital gains tax (CGT) and stamp duty, whereas cash gifts are generally tax free. Centrelink recipients should check the rules for maximum gift amounts and time frames.

Margaret received an offer of a parental guarantee from her parents. Her maximum loan amount was $600 000 and she had a pre-approval to buy for $600 000 using a parental guarantee rather than a deposit.

She found a property for $800 000. As Margaret's maximum loan amount was $600 000, her parents offered to give her the $200 000 from their investments. The parental guarantee was no longer needed because the loan amount of $600 000 was now only 75 per cent of the property value.

An alternative to gifting is a formal loan agreement. This can impact the borrower's borrowing capacity. However, if the loan doesn't need to be repaid until the sale of the property some lenders will consider this without it impacting servicing. This is ideal if your parents wish to provide funds without permanently gifting them.

Kai and Jenny wanted to buy a home near their family but couldn't afford it on their salaries. Their parents offered a substantial $500 000 contribution as a formal loan. No repayments were required, but the parents would receive the funds back upon sale or via their estate if they died before the property was sold.

Details:

- Purchase price: $1 500 000
- Parent loan: $500 000 (no repayments until sale)
- Loan amount needed: $1 000 000 (67 per cent of property value).

This arrangement allowed Kai and Jenny to live near family without needing a deposit. Their parents benefited from having them close by, without creating an unfair advantage for one child over their siblings. They obtained legal advice, a formal loan contract was drawn up, and Kai and Jenny felt comfortable managing repayments on their $1 000 000 loan.

Favourable purchases

A favourable purchase occurs when you buy a property from a family member, or sometimes a close friend, at a price below the property's market value. It's called a favourable purchase because the 'favour' is the difference between what the property is worth and what you pay for it.

In certain circumstances, some lenders will allow the loan to be assessed on the 'market valuation', rather than the contract price. When structured correctly, this can allow the buyer to purchase with a small deposit or, depending on the valuation, no deposit at all.

Favourable purchases are most common in family situations including:

- estate-planning scenarios
- intergenerational wealth transfers
- downsizing parents helping adult children into the market.

A common example is where a property is part of a deceased estate and is sold at a discounted price to the next generation. Another is a parent selling their home to a child at a reduced price so they can downsize while providing support.

Why lenders may allow a loan with no deposit

From a lender's perspective, the key risk is the LVR. If a property is worth more than the purchase price, the buyer effectively has equity from day one. In many cases, this equity can replace the need for a traditional cash deposit.

However, not all banks treat favourable purchases the same way and policies vary. The structure, valuation, relationship between the buyer and seller, and the documentation matter. Advice and the correct lender are crucial here.

Dave and Ivana planned to support their adult son Luca with a parental guarantee. He had completed his degree, started full-time work and saved close to $60 000 while living at home during his university years. They were confident in his spending habits and long-term mindset and were comfortable helping him enter the market.

Despite working full time and having minimal living expenses, Luca's income limited his borrowing capacity. On his own, he could only afford a unit or townhouse. While these options may suit some buyers, they didn't align with his longer term wealth goals so he wanted to see if his borrowing power could be improved.

Rather than gifting cash, his parents explored an alternative strategy. They owned an investment property purchased in 2018 for $500 000. By 2025, the property had increased in value to approximately $800 000. They agreed on a purchase price of $600 000, effectively reflecting the original purchase cost plus associated expenses.

Luca made a favourable purchase. He purchased the home from his parents using a bank loan. He then rented the property out. His loan covered the amount his parents owed on the property. The bank loaned him 100 per cent of the purchase plus costs because they relied on the valuation of the property being $800 000 rather than the actual purchase price ($600 000). His loan was 100 per cent of the purchase price but only 75 per cent of the valuation of the property.

By structuring the transaction this way, the loan represented 75 per cent of the property's value. This meant Luca didn't have to contribute a cash deposit and could retain his savings in an offset account for flexibility and security.

Key figures:

- Property value: $800 000
- Purchase price: $600 000
- Purchase costs: $35 000 (stamp duty payable as an investment)
- Deposit required: $0 (savings used to cover costs)
- Loan amount: $600 000 (100 per cent of purchase price, 75 per cent of value)

(continued)

- Mortgage repayment: $3407 per month (P&I, 5.5 per cent, 30 years)
- Market rent: $750 per week.

This structure enabled Luca to enter the market earlier, preserve his cash and position himself to use the equity in the future—either to upgrade to a family home or continue investing. For Dave and Ivana, it provided a way to support their hardworking son without compromising their own financial position.

Many parents aren't aware of strategies like favourable purchases or how equity can be used creatively without handing over cash. As with any approach, the key is understanding the options available so decisions can be made that genuinely suit the family's goals and circumstances.

Be smart and layer up!

You can use some or all of the strategies discussed in this chapter to enter the property market. For example, you might use the FHSS scheme to help build your deposit, live rent-free with family and combine this with state-based stamp-duty concessions or the Australian Government 5% Deposit Scheme. Often, it's the smart combination of these options, rather than relying on just one, that's most effective.

Nicole lived rent free with her parents while saving for her first property and built up $60 000, which in 2019 was enough to get started. Her plan was to buy a property to live in for 12 months purely to qualify for the stamp-duty concession, saving her around $20 000.

However, when she compared the numbers, it became clear that moving into the property didn't make financial sense. The rental income she would forgo, combined with her increased living costs, outweighed the stamp-duty savings, particularly at a time when the Australian Government 5% Deposit Scheme didn't yet exist. Staying at home, which was her preference anyway, was the stronger option.

Nicole's main obstacle was the deposit. For a $600 000 investment purchase, she needed about $85 000 as a 10 per cent deposit, plus costs (approximately $10 000 in LMI)—or about $145 000 to avoid LMI altogether. After seeing the scenarios, her parents offered a limited parental guarantee so she could move forward without having to leave home. Nicole contributed her $60 000 and her parents' guarantee covered the shortfall up to $85 000.

By 2021, the property was valued at $850 000. Nicole was able to remove the parental guarantee and, at the same time, use the equity she had built to purchase a second investment property

(continued)

interstate for $700 000. By 2025, her two investment properties looked like this:

* The first, purchased for $600 000, was worth approximately $900 000.
* The second, purchased for $700 000, was worth around $820 000.

In total, Nicole had built approximately $420 000 in equity from an initial $60 000 deposit with a parental guarantee that was in place for less than two years.

In 2025, Nicole and her partner decided to buy a home to live in together near her parents—something that would have been far more difficult without her earlier investment strategy. They chose to sell one investment property to upgrade their home and retained the other as a long-term investment. While Nicole ultimately forwent the stamp-duty concession, she had successfully leveraged free accommodation and a parental guarantee to build a strong foundation and create long-term flexibility.

There are many ways for families to help their children into the property market. The best course of action is to have a joint appointment with a mortgage broker. Have an open and honest conversation where everyone talks about what's important to them and ask the broker to prepare possible scenarios. Become informed so you don't miss out on potential opportunities. You might just be able to enter the market faster or in a way you didn't know existed!

Start with this . . .

Stop for a minute and identify some things to research or discuss with your mortgage broker:

* Which schemes or grants might you be able to apply for?
* Have you considered a more unconventional buying route like buying with a friend, family member or parental guarantor?

5

Deciding on your strategy: Buying a home to live in

As a first-home buyer you'll not only face big decisions like what you'll buy, but also the strategy you'll adopt to buy it. Will you purchase a home to live in straight away, or will you take the investor route, renting where you want to live and buying where you can afford, while your property quietly works for you in the background? Both strategies come with unique opportunities and challenges. The decision is not just about numbers — it's about lifestyle, timing, your values and what's actually possible in your situation.

By this stage, you may have a clearer sense of the options available to you. That clarity might have narrowed your choices or opened up ideas you hadn't considered. Perhaps your goal is to buy a family home, but reaching it means moving to a different suburb, or even another city. Maybe your deposit limitations make building a home the best option, especially with government incentives. You could have decided that you love city life and will invest regionally while renting in the city, or perhaps a parental guarantee allows you to stay at home a bit longer while purchasing an investment property elsewhere. Whatever path you take, the key is understanding the trade-offs and opportunities in your specific situation before making the leap.

Whatever your situation, you need a strategy for your first property, not just a vague dream. This strategy will be built off the back of your 'why', which is why we started with that back in chapter 1. Once you're clear on your strategy, it becomes much easier to choose the right property and the right path to get into the market. Ultimately, this is about finding the best way possible to achieve your personal goals.

In this chapter, we focus on the option of buying a home to live in (also known as an owner-occupied home). We'll go into the emotional traps, the practical strategy and how to make good decisions without losing your mind in the process.

Your first home is a step, not the final destination

Buying your first home is one of those rare moments in life where excitement and uncertainty collide. You're imagining the life you'll build there, while also trying to make sense of a process that can feel bigger and more complex than you expected.

Almost every first-home buyer begins in the same place: hopeful, overwhelmed and wondering if they are making the right decisions. That's normal. You're not behind, you're not weird and you're not the only one who opens a real estate app at 11.30 pm, zooms out on the map and thinks, 'Is it too late to move to Wagga?'

This chapter is here to help you navigate that feeling. You'll learn how to:

- understand your priorities and your non-negotiables
- manage the emotional rollercoaster of the buying process
- communicate with the right people and ignore the noise
- balance your lifestyle goals with long-term financial sense.

As the average first-home buyer age rises, more Aussies are entering the market in their 30s and 40s, often with very different lives than buyers a decade earlier. You might have kids, pets or simply want more space and stability. And because you didn't buy a small 'starter place' in your 20s, it can feel like you've missed a step and deserve to jump straight into the dream family home. That feeling is completely valid, but it's also where many buyers get stuck.

Buying a home isn't just a financial transaction—it's a decision that shapes your lifestyle, your sense of security and your long-term wealth. But your first home is rarely your forever home. Most owner-occupiers move again within a few years as their needs, incomes and families evolve, so release the pressure to get it perfect (breathe in, breathe out, release that tension in your shoulders). You're not locking yourself into a lifelong contract with a three-bedroom brick veneer—you're choosing the next chapter that gets you closer to the life you want.

Emotional traps for first-home buyers

When you're buying a place to live in, emotions are everywhere. That's completely understandable. The goal is not to switch off your emotions, but to make sure they're not the ones driving the car while your logic is tied up in the boot. Here are five common emotional traps owner-occupiers fall into and how to avoid them.

The dream home myth (and the 'forever home' fantasy)

Most first-home buyers secretly want their first home to tick every box. Light, bright, renovated, close to everything, quiet street, great neighbours, north-facing backyard, walk-in pantry, subway tiles and of course 'future proofed'. Here we are to burst your bubble: your first home may not be perfect. You might get most of your needs met and only some of your wants. That's not failure, that's normal.

Having a detailed dream home in mind can create a few problems. You might overstretch your budget and box yourself into stressful repayments; or delay buying for years, waiting for something 'perfect' while prices and rents keep moving. You might talk yourself out of good, solid options because they are 7 out of 10 instead of a mythical 12 out of 10.

We strongly encourage you to remove the phrase 'forever home' from your vocabulary for now. It piles on unnecessary pressure. You don't need to lock in the perfect home for every version of your future self; you just need a home that works well for you for the next reasonable season of life.

Fear of making a mistake

Fear is one of the strongest emotions you'll feel when buying a home. Fear is normal, but it's not a great decision maker. The antidote to fear is good data and clear criteria. There's a reason the old acronym for fear is '**f**alse **e**vidence **a**ppearing **r**eal'. Your job is to replace false evidence with real evidence.

Fear can look like:

- *What if I buy in the wrong place?*
  Spend time in the suburb, talk to locals, walk the streets at different times of day. Look at school catchments, access to transport, flood maps and council plans. If you turn up and next door has three abandoned cars in the front yard and a lawn that hasn't been mowed since 2014, that's useful evidence.

- *What if the market falls?*
  When you buy an owner-occupied home, your primary driver is security and lifestyle, not short-term speculation. Property values will rise and fall in the short term, but you're not buying to hold for three years then flip. You're buying a stable base for your life.

- *What if there's something wrong with the property?*
  That's where due diligence comes in. Building and pest inspections, strata reports, checking council records and having a good conveyancer are all about turning fear into facts. We deal with the buying process and due diligence in detail in later chapters, but for now, remember: don't ignore red flags and don't skip checks because you're 'too in love' with the house.

Comparing yourself with others

We talked about this in chapter 1, but it's especially common for first-home buyers. Comparison will try to sneak into every part of your home-buying journey. It might be friends who bought years earlier in a nicer suburb. It might be family members who keep reminding you what they paid for their first home in 1994. It might be social-media feeds full of perfectly styled homes that don't even look lived in. The trouble with comparison is you don't know how much help they had from family, how much debt they're carrying behind the scenes or what compromises they made elsewhere in their life to get there.

Your job is to build a life on your terms, not to recreate someone else's highlight reel. If you're in a relationship, you both need to be strong on this. Decide together what's right for your values, your budget and your lifestyle — and stay in your lane.

Emotional pressure from family

Family can be one of the biggest emotional influences on your first-home purchase. Often it comes from a good place, but it can still be unhelpful. Your parents or extended family may have bought in a completely different era, with different prices, different interest rates and very different expectations about what a 'proper home' looks like. They might insist that you 'must' buy a three-bedroom brick home on a big block because they would never have bought an apartment or a townhouse.

Their reality is not your reality. Today, many buyers can't afford to live close to family and buy a huge family home off the bat. You might need to move further out, buy a smaller place, choose a townhouse or unit, or live somewhere different from where your parents think you 'should' live. Listen respectfully, but remember you're the one making the repayments. Advice that ignores your actual numbers and your strategy is not advice you have to take.

Falling in love too fast

Falling in love with a property is incredibly common. You walk in, the sun is streaming through the kitchen window, there's a pot of basil on the bench, someone's baked bread, the styling is immaculate and suddenly you're saying things like, 'I could see us here forever'. That feeling isn't the enemy, but it does need boundaries. When you lead with emotion, it becomes much easier to overlook red flags, push your budget beyond what's actually comfortable or compromise on things that genuinely matter all in the name of 'this feels right'.

As a general rule, Mercury and Venus don't need to align when you inspect your first property. In fact, it's usually better if they don't. Visit a range of properties in your price bracket so you know what's normal before you fall hard for one. Then come back to your strategy and your list of deal-breakers before making any offers.

Building your owner-occupier strategy

Once you've named the emotional traps, you can start to build a proper strategy for buying a home to live in. Your owner-occupier strategy rises and falls on two things:

1. Can you genuinely afford to live there — not just on paper, but in real life — over the next three to five years?
2. Does the property support your goals and lifestyle for that same period?

To answer those questions, it helps to think in three layers:

- hard considerations: the non-negotiable numbers and property details
- soft considerations: lifestyle and liveability
- deal-breakers: your red lines.

Hard considerations

Hard considerations are the financial realities that have to work. If they don't, the whole plan collapses. Start with your borrowing capacity and whether it actually gets you into the suburbs or property types you're targeting. From there, look closely at the monthly repayments at today's interest rates and consider what happens if rates rise. Owning a home also comes with ongoing costs: council rates, strata or body corporate fees, home insurance and maintenance. All this needs to fit comfortably within your budget.

You also need to understand the mechanics of your deposit. Do you have enough saved, or will you rely on a parental guarantee or LMI to bridge the gap? And importantly, once the dust settles on the purchase, can you still afford the life you want over the next three to five years—travel, having kids, changing careers or studying—without feeling financially squeezed?

This is why focusing solely on your maximum borrowing capacity is dangerous. That number reflects the bank's risk tolerance, not your lifestyle or stress levels. You need to draw your own line in the sand, your personal upper limit, where you can say, 'Yes, we could technically borrow more, but we're choosing not to'.

There may also need to be a hard consideration of the number of rooms and whether you need a yard for a dog. The size of the yard and the type of property may flow into your soft considerations.

Soft considerations

Soft considerations are the lifestyle factors that influence how happy you will be living there day to day. These are not trivial. They're often the difference between loving your home and resenting it. Soft considerations might include:

- preferred suburbs or postcodes
- commute time to work or study

- access to public transport, shops, cafes, parks or beaches
- minimum number of bedrooms and bathrooms
- type of dwelling: house, townhouse, villa, unit or apartment
- parking and storage: garage, carport, on-street parking, storage cage
- noise levels and general feel of the street and neighbourhood.

These factors are flexible, but they aren't meaningless. If you choose a home that clashes with your lifestyle, you'll feel it every single day. It might show up as constant rushing, long commutes, isolation from your community or the feeling that you never really settled in.

Deal-breakers

Deal-breakers are your hard 'no' items: the guardrails that stop you from making decisions you'll regret later. They sit beneath all your other considerations as the final filter: the lines you simply won't cross, no matter how charming the property or persuasive the agent. For some buyers this might mean refusing to buy with an LVR above 90 per cent, avoiding anything on a main road, steering clear of a two-bedroom apartment with only one bathroom or saying no to a fibro house that screams 'future money pit'.

Think of your deal-breakers like a driving test. Some mistakes are minor. Forgetting to indicate once might not fail you. But if you run a red light, it's an instant fail. In the same way, a property might have a few minor compromises, but once it hits a certain threshold of issues, or crosses a red line, you walk away.

Property in action

Stop for a minute and write down your own *hard considerations, soft considerations and deal-breakers*. Take the time to dig into what your needs and wants are and take these notes with you as you review properties to ensure you stay in line with your goals. One person's hard consideration or deal-breaker is someone else's soft consideration.

In chapter 8, you'll find a spreadsheet that you can download and use for your own property search (see table 8.1). While it's designed for owner-occupier buyers, you can also use it if you're buying an investment property.

You may need to inspect some properties that don't meet your criteria. This will give you a greater sense of price, features and what's right for you in the markets you're looking at.

Growth and resale potential

Even though this will be your home first and foremost, not an investment, it's still smart to consider who might buy it from you one day. You don't want to ignore basic investment fundamentals. Think about whether the property sits in a desirable school zone for future buyers; whether the area is improving, stagnant or declining; and whether any major developments nearby could help, or hurt, property values. You should also consider if there's anything about the property itself that might put off a large portion of potential buyers, such as an unusual layout, small land size or a very busy road. Taking these factors into account now helps protect your future options without taking away from your enjoyment of the home today.

Property coach and Rach's fellow host on the *this is property* show ('wink') John Pidgeon often talks about three main ways to make money in property:

- Buy at a discount.
- Add value.
- Let time and capital growth do the heavy lifting.

With an owner-occupied home you might not hit all three, but it's worth seeing if you can achieve at least two. For example, you might pay close to market value, but add value through cosmetic renovations while letting time and growth do their thing. Or you might secure the property at a slight discount and later add a granny flat or extension because the block size allows it. You don't need to treat your home like a full-blown development project, but you also don't want to buy something that will be hard to sell later.

Emotional fit

Numbers matter, but you also have to live in this place. Emotional fit is simply asking yourself, 'Can I see myself living well here?' It's the part where you consider how the home aligns with your lifestyle, routines and sense of comfort. A single person might value security and feel most at ease in an apartment building with secure access rather than a freestanding house. A couple planning a family may care more about a safe backyard, a quiet street and access to parks. Someone who works from home might prioritise natural light and a practical layout over being close to the office.

Emotional fit isn't a free pass to ignore your budget or override your deal-breakers, it's the final layer you test once the numbers and fundamentals already make sense. It's about choosing a home that not only works on paper, but also supports the way you actually want to live.

Know your numbers

Before you get attached to any property, you need to know your numbers clearly. That includes:

- your borrowing power and how it was calculated
- your realistic monthly repayments at current rates and at slightly higher rates
- your personal borrowing limit, which may be lower than the bank's maximum
- extra ownership costs such as rates, water, strata or body corporate, insurance and maintenance
- one-off purchase costs like stamp duty, legal fees and inspections.

This is where your mortgage broker or lender is a key part of your property team. Ask questions until you fully understand the numbers. If you feel pressured to borrow more than you're comfortable with, slow things down. *You* are in charge of your risk tolerance — not the bank, not your broker, not your parents.

Who is your sounding board?

If this is your first property purchase, having a sounding board can be incredibly valuable. This is someone you can bounce ideas off, who will help keep you grounded and logical. Your sounding board might be a trusted friend who has bought property before, a family member who understands your situation without trying to relive their own glory days through you, a mortgage broker or adviser who can give you an unemotional view of the numbers, or even a buyer's agent or property coach if that fits your budget and goals.

What you don't want is someone who is chronically negative and constantly talking you out of everything, or someone reckless who keeps saying, 'Just go for it, you only live once'. You also want to avoid anyone projecting their own regrets or fears onto your decisions. The goal isn't to have someone tell you what to do; it's to have someone help you think clearly, weigh your options and stay anchored when the excitement or stress of buying your first home starts to take over.

Prepare for the emotional rollercoaster

Buying your first home isn't a calm, predictable journey; it's a rollercoaster. You'll swing between excitement and nerves, hope and disappointment, frustration and empowerment. Some days you'll feel completely overwhelmed; other days you'll feel unstoppable. And it's perfectly normal to cycle through several of these emotions in the same week, or even within the same afternoon. Recognising this ahead of time helps you stay grounded and reminds you that nothing is wrong, you're simply experiencing what every first-time buyer goes through.

Knowing this in advance helps. When you hit a low patch, you can remind yourself, 'This is part of the process, not a sign that I am failing'. The key is to keep coming back to your strategy, your numbers and your deal-breakers, rather than letting emotions take the wheel.

Start with your own clarity, not real-estate apps

Most first-home buyers start their search backwards. They open a real estate app, look at everything that's for sale and then try to figure out their budget, strategy and non-negotiables on the fly. That's like doing the groceries while you're starving. You walk in with no plan, grab things you don't need and spend more than you intended.

When you go to the supermarket, three things help you stay in control:

- a full stomach so you're not shopping hungry
- a clear list of what you actually need
- a budget.

The same applies to property. Your 'full stomach' is emotional clarity: you're not trying to fix your entire life with one house and you understand your values and your time frame. Your 'list' is the combination of your needs, wants and deal-breakers, giving you a clear filter for what truly matters. And your 'budget' is the realistic price range based on your actual numbers, not your fantasies or the borrowing limit the bank waves at you. Once you have those, then you open the apps. Now you're searching with purpose rather than scrolling in chaos.

Needs vs wants

One of the most powerful exercises you can do is to clearly separate your genuine needs from your wants. Needs are the features your home must have in order to support your lifestyle in a meaningful way. Wants are preferences that would be nice, but you can live without. Examples of needs might be:

- enough natural light for you to feel comfortable at home
- reasonable distance to work, study, family or other key locations
- a layout that works for how you actually live, not just how it looks in photos
- a minimum number of bedrooms or bathrooms
- affordable strata levies if you're buying into a complex.

Examples of wants might be:

- a fully renovated kitchen
- a pool
- a particular street that is slightly closer to the beach
- a specific style of façade or interior finish.

A simple question to help sort the list is: *If I remove this feature, would this home still support my lifestyle in a meaningful way?*

If yes, it's a want.

If not, it's a need.

You'll be surprised how much clarity this brings. It also makes it easier to compare properties fairly, rather than getting dazzled by styling or surface level features.

When your needs don't match the market

For many first-home buyers, there comes a moment where the numbers and the wish list don't line up. Your budget says one thing, your needs list says another and the local market shrugs and says, 'good luck'.

When that happens, you have a few levers you can pull:

- *Revisit your suburbs*. Can you move one or two rings further out and still have a lifestyle you're happy with?
- *Revisit your dwelling type*. Could you live happily in a townhouse or unit instead of a freestanding house?
- *Revisit your needs and wants*. Are there any 'needs' that are actually 'wants' in disguise?
- *Revisit timing or strategy*. Is it more realistic to rent where you want to live and buy an investment property somewhere more affordable for now?

Sometimes you can solve the problem by adjusting one or two variables. Other times, you realise that buying an owner-occupied home right now, in your preferred area, isn't realistic. That's not the end of the story. It just might mean shifting to an investing-first strategy, which we'll turn our attention to in chapter 6. The key is to be honest with yourself. A home that looks perfect but leaves you stressed, resentful and financially stretched isn't actually a good fit.

Turning emotions into clear decisions

By the time you're actively inspecting properties, it will feel like there's a lot coming at you at once: agents calling, emails arriving, inspections, auctions, friends giving opinions, family sending you links at 6 am. To stay grounded, you need a way to turn your emotions into clear, binary decisions.

A practical approach is to:

- write down your five core needs and five key wants
- write down your non-negotiable deal-breakers.

Assess each property you're seriously considering against this framework and ask:

- Does it meet the hard considerations?
- Does it meet enough of the soft considerations?
- Does it cross any deal-breakers?

If a property fails a deal-breaker, it's a no, even if you have a good feeling about it. If it passes the framework, then you can give more weight to the emotional fit. Over time, this process turns what can feel like a messy emotional fog into a clear 'yes' or 'no'. It's not about removing emotion completely. It's about making sure emotion and logic are working together, rather than against each other.

Start with this...

Take a moment to consider the following:

* If you're a first-home buyer, how emotional are you, and are your feelings driving the decision? How can you keep your emotions in check?
* Are you surrounded by others who are giving you 'advice'? How can you respond to them respectfully, while staying on target for your goals?
* What concerns you about buying your first home, and what research can you do to calm that fear?

6

Deciding on your strategy: Buying an investment property

Buying your first property as an investment is currently one of the most powerful pathways into the market. For many first-home buyers, this isn't where they expected to end up, but sometimes this is where the numbers and the lifestyle factors point. You usually arrive at this option via one of two ways:

1. *You deliberately choose to be an investor first.* You're happy to keep renting or living at home for a while and you want your first property to be a stepping stone for wealth rather than a place you personally live in.

2. *You realise it's not realistic to buy where you want to live.* You always imagined buying a home to live in, but you've worked through the hard considerations in earlier chapters and know the timing for your first home to live in isn't right. You still want to own property, so by default you're looking at becoming a landlord and buying an investment property elsewhere.

Both paths are valid. In both cases, the goal is the same: you want your first property to move you forward financially, not box you in. Just like buying an owner-occupied home, this path isn't only about spreadsheets and interest rates. It's emotional. You're dealing with uncertainty, bigger numbers than you've ever handled and a decision you can't undo easily. On top of that, you're adding an extra layer: tenants, property managers, vacancies and all the fun of being a landlord for the first time. There's a whole mindset and perspective shift that comes with this.

It's not uncommon to experience a little bit of fear around this concept. Fears for first-time investors include:

- picking the wrong property
- fear of bad tenants
- fear of overpaying
- fear of long vacancy periods
- fear of making a big mistake that you can't fix quickly.

If you're the first person in your family to buy an investment property, these fears can be even louder. You'll probably have people telling you it's too risky, too hard or something only 'rich' people do. None of that is necessarily true. The way to reduce the uncertainty is not to avoid decisions, it's to become as informed as you can be, set a clear strategy and build a team around you so you're not flying blind.

In this chapter we'll explore:

- why buying as an investor often means going 'borderless'
- how to match your strategy to your lending and your life
- how to research locations without relying on guesswork or hype
- common cautions for your first investment property
- the basics of rentvesting and freevesting
- being an ethical landlord, not a greedy caricature
- how ownership structures and title types fit into your overall strategy
- how to understand the property cycle so you're investing with knowledge.

Sounds like a lot, doesn't it? Don't worry: by the end of the chapter, you should have a clear sense of whether an investment-first strategy suits you and if so, how to approach it with confidence rather than chaos.

When Australia becomes borderless

Regardless of whether you set out from day one to buy an investment property, or you can't afford to buy where you live, there's a good chance your first property won't be in the suburb where you currently live.

Once you decide to become an investor first, your mindset has to change. This decision often means leaving your postcode, and when you accept that, Australia becomes borderless. You now have thousands of micro markets to consider, not just the three suburbs you drive through on the way to work. The upside is choice and opportunity; the downside is more complexity and the need for better research.

It's also worth pointing out that your first property will always feel risky, whether it's an investment or a home to live in. You've never done this before, so your brain labels it as unknown. An investment property will likely be somewhere you can't drive past easily, it will have tenants, and you'll have to trust professionals such as property managers and local trades. That adds layers to the emotional load. Because of this, you can't afford to wing it. You need a clear strategy first, and to then find the property that fits that strategy—not the other way around.

Strategy matching

When people talk about research, they often jump straight to suburb lists, 'hotspot' articles or social media tips. That's not research—that's *content.*

Proper research starts with strategy matching. You need to line up four moving parts:

- your goals and time frame
- your borrowing capacity and cash flow
- location fundamentals
- property type and asset quality.

If these four parts don't match, you can end up with a property that looks good on paper, but doesn't move you towards your goals.

Goals and time frame

Before you look at any listings, you need to answer two basic questions: What is this investment for? What is my investing goal?

Some common goals include:

- *long-term capital growth*: you want to hold the property for 10 years or more, ride the ups and downs, and build equity over time
- *cash flow*: you want the rent to cover most or all of the holding costs and you value a stronger yield even if capital growth is slower
- *tax benefits as a supporting factor*: you may claim interest, expenses and depreciation, but tax benefits support the strategy — they're not the entire strategy
- *a stepping stone*: you want this property to help you buy a home to live in, or to leverage into a second investment later on.

You don't need to have a perfectly detailed 30-year plan, but you do need a clear primary goal. Buying 'just because everyone says property is good' isn't a strategy.

Borrowing capacity and cash flow

Next, you need to understand your borrowing capacity as an investor and how the numbers shift compared with buying a home to live in. A few key things work differently. Your rental income is usually included in your borrowing calculations, but lenders will 'shade' that income — meaning they only count a portion of the expected rent rather than the full amount. Investment loans can also attract slightly higher interest rates than owner-occupied loans, which changes your repayments and long-term cash flow. And your bank or broker will want to see that you can comfortably handle vacancies, rising interest rates and general property expenses without tipping into financial stress. This broader lens helps ensure you're not just able to *buy* the investment, you're able to *hold* it.

On top of the loan itself, you must understand the ongoing cost to hold the property. This includes:

- interest repayments
- council rates and water
- strata or body corporate fees, if relevant
- land tax if it applies in your state
- landlord insurance
- property management fees
- a realistic allowance for maintenance and repairs
- allowance for some vacancy across the year.

'Purchase price' and 'cost to hold' are not the same thing. Two properties could each cost $800 000, but if one rents for $350/week and the other rents for $900/week, the ongoing cost to you will be very different. This is where your accountant is important. Your true cost to hold can only be calculated once you factor in tax deductions, depreciation and your personal tax rate. A good accountant can model realistic cash flow scenarios so that you're not guessing.

Location fundamentals

Once your goals and lending are clear, you can look at location. Remember, as an investor you may be buying somewhere you would never choose to live personally. That's fine, because you aren't going to live there.

Some things to research when comparing locations include:

- *Growth corridors*
  Look for regions that have shown consistent population growth and increasing demand over time. These 'growth corridors' often benefit from people moving for lifestyle, affordability or employment reasons. In recent decades, places like Wollongong, Newcastle, Ballarat, Geelong, the Sunshine Coast and Toowoomba have all seen strong demand driven by shifting population patterns.

- *Major infrastructure spending*
  Pay attention to where governments and large institutions are investing. New hospitals, rail extensions, universities, industrial hubs, defence bases and major road upgrades can all support long-term demand. Infrastructure attracts jobs, improves liveability and can fundamentally change how desirable an area becomes over time.

- *Economic diversity*
  Consider how resilient the local economy is. Areas that rely heavily on a single industry, like mining towns, can offer great yields during boom times but fall sharply when the industry slows. In contrast, regions with multiple employers and varied sectors tend to have more stable employment and housing demand, which can support more consistent long-term growth.

- *Supply of new land*
  Think about how easily new housing can be built. Some areas have limited land, which naturally restricts supply and can help support growth. Others have endless available land and

large greenfield estates where thousands of similar homes are built at once. Oversupply in these areas can weigh down both price growth and rental demand.

- *Tightness of the rental market*
  Investigate vacancy rates, both now and historically. A vacancy rate shows what percentage of rental properties are sitting empty at a given time. As a rough rule, many investors prefer areas that have stayed below about 3 per cent over the long term. Short spikes aren't always a problem, but extended periods of high vacancy can signal risk.
  Vacancy rate data is publicly available on free websites like SQM Research, and is often searchable by suburb or postcode. Look back five to ten years to understand the pattern, how often the market has been tight, how often it has softened and whether the current moment reflects a long-term trend or just a short-term blip.

Property type and asset quality

The final part of strategy matching is *property type*. This is where many first-time investors get caught out. A common mistake is to chase yield alone. Someone sees a tiny studio apartment with a seemingly great rental return for the purchase price and thinks, 'This is amazing'. They don't stop to ask why the price hasn't moved for 15 years, or why banks are nervous about lending on certain small apartments.

Your property type should fit both your goals and the location. For example, a house with a granny flat in a regional centre might offer stronger yield and the ability to rent to two sets of tenants. A villa or townhouse in an established suburb might offer a balance of capital growth and yield. A freestanding house on a decent block in a growth corridor might have stronger long-term growth potential, even if the yield is modest at first.

We delve more deeply into asset types in chapter 7, but for now remember this: you aren't buying a brochure. You're buying a physical asset with a real-world history and future. Look past the glossy marketing to the fundamentals.

Reducing your risks

Your first investment property doesn't have to be perfect, but it does need to be sensible. One way to reduce risk is to write a list of potential issues to look out for when you're viewing properties.

Here are some we're always cautious about.

Small studio apartments in high-rise buildings

Studios can look attractive on yield. The rent looks high compared with the price. The problem is that many of these properties have had almost no capital growth in 15 years or more and some are still selling for less than their original purchase price. Lenders can also be stricter with small apartments, which limits your buyer pool in the future.

Off-the-plan high-rise apartments

Buying off the plan can involve an 18- to 24-month — or longer — build window. Your 10 per cent deposit is tied up while you earn little or no return and a lot can change in that time. Interest rates, lending rules, your job, your health or the broader market can all shift before settlement. You also can't rely on a standard pre-approval for an off-the-plan purchase. Pre-approvals generally last around three months, which is useless for an 18-month build. For a first-time investor, the added complexity and risk are rarely worth it.

Properties with major known headaches

For a first investment, be cautious about buying places that come with obvious high maintenance or structural risks, such as:

- large, old retaining walls that already show signs of movement
- private swimming pools and spas
- old fibro shacks that haven't been updated and may contain asbestos
- fireplaces that may not meet current rental safety rules in your state.

All properties have some maintenance, but if you can avoid obvious dramas on property number one, you'll make your life much easier.

Single-industry or speculative locations

Be very cautious about towns that rely on a single industry, particularly mining towns where yields look incredible on paper. Everything looks great until it isn't. If you want your first property to be a relatively low drama stepping stone, you'll usually want a location with multiple industries and a stable underlying population.

Large new estates where almost everyone is an investor

A new pocket inside an established suburb can be fine, but a brand new suburb where almost every buyer is an investor can be risky. You might end up competing with hundreds of similar properties for tenants, and rents may soften if too many investors try to undercut each other.

Overall, your first investment property should be as 'turn key' and boring as possible. Ideally, you want a property that someone can move into tomorrow. It might be an existing home with a long-term tenant already in place, or a new build that's finished and ready to lease, not a speculative off-the-plan purchase or a half-finished renovation that depends on your weekends and a miracle.

Your investor dream team

In chapter 9, we'll talk about assembling your property team. But we'd like to mention here that as an investor, there are a few extra people you may want in your corner:

- A good accountant who understands property
- A mortgage broker who can model different scenarios as your portfolio grows
- A property coach or investment-focused adviser, if your budget allows
- A buyer's agent who works specifically with investors, if you choose to outsource some of the research
- A quality property manager in the local area.

Before you make any offers, it's worth running potential properties past at least your accountant and a local property manager. The accountant can help you understand tax implications, depreciation and cash flow. The property manager can give you a realistic view of rent, likely tenant demand and any quirks of the area that you won't see in a listing.

Factors to consider when becoming a landlord

Becoming a landlord for the first time isn't only a financial decision—it's also a psychological and practical one. Let's have a look at some key factors to consider.

Adopting the psychology of being a landlord

You have to be comfortable with the idea that other people will live in your asset and that sometimes things will go wrong. Tenants may damage something. Appliances will break. A storm might rip a fence down. You need to have enough emotional bandwidth to handle the occasional email from your property manager asking for a decision or approval to spend money.

Being involved

Even with a good property manager, you still have to make decisions, read emails and approve quotes. Investment property ownership isn't a completely set-and-forget situation, particularly if you have more than one property over time.

Giving up first-home-buyer concessions

When you buy your first property as an investment, you'll often miss out on owner-occupier incentives such as first-home-buyer grants and stamp-duty concessions. Many people automatically assume this is a bad move. It isn't that simple.

You may be able to buy an investment property with a smaller deposit sooner than if you waited to save more and access a grant or scheme for an owner-occupied home. By the time you saved that extra deposit, property prices in your target area may have grown faster than your savings. Forgoing $25 000 to $30 000 of grants might be worth it if it gets you the right asset years earlier. The interest on the investment loan may also be tax deductible and depreciation may improve your after-tax position.

The key is to model both scenarios with a broker and an accountant so that you make an informed decision, not a decision based on fear-of-missing-out on government incentives.

CAPITAL GAINS TAX (CGT)

Investment properties are subject to CGT when you sell for more than what you paid for the property. That's the aim. Before you buy, talk to your accountant about how CGT would apply to your strategy, especially if you think you may sell within a certain time frame. There could also be factors to consider if you're a couple buying an investment property in joint names.

DEPRECIATION AND TAX BENEFITS

Depreciation is a big part of the investment puzzle. It can significantly reduce your taxable income from the property, which improves your cash flow after tax.

> If you're buying for investment, a tax depreciation schedule is a game changer. This is a detailed report prepared by a qualified quantity surveyor that shows how much you can claim in depreciation on your investment property each year.
>
> You can usually expect a tax depreciation schedule to cost somewhere in the range of $500 to $900 as a one-off fee and it can last for up to 40 years for that property.

(continued)

A simple example:

- A house has $500 000 in construction cost (known as Division 43 capital works). That component is depreciated at 2.5 per cent per year over 40 years. In year one, that's $12 500 of capital works deductions.
- On top of that, there may be deductions for Division 40 (fixtures and fittings) of, say, $7500 per year.

In total, that's $20 000 of depreciation in a year. If the owner is on a 37 per cent marginal tax rate, the tax saving from that depreciation alone is $7400 for the year. Many people mistakenly believe depreciation schedules are only worthwhile for brand-new properties. While the savings can be higher on new or newly renovated properties, schedules are still valuable for many existing homes.

Here are some quick guidelines:

- *New properties:* no brainer. You can usually claim both the building and the fittings and fixtures.
- *Properties built after 1987:* often worth a report because in many cases you can still claim the building.
- *Older properties that have been renovated:* also worth checking. Even if the original structure is old, renovations and improvements may be claimable.

Always check with a quantity surveyor and your accountant to confirm whether a depreciation schedule is appropriate for your property.

CASH RESERVES

You should have a buffer for maintenance, unexpected repairs and some vacancy. If the hot water system dies and you don't have any savings, that's a problem. A sensible buffer helps you stay in the game when life happens.

Rentvesting basics

If you've ever thought, 'It's impossible to buy a home where I want to live', or if you love your current lifestyle but still want to be in the property market, rentvesting might be for you.

Rentvesting is where you rent the home you live in—often in an area or dwelling type you couldn't afford—and you purchase an investment property in a different location that better fits your budget and strategy. Once you decide to rentvest, the map opens up. You stop looking at property solely as 'my home' and start seeing it as a tool for building wealth. Emotionally, that can be a big shift. You're choosing lifestyle with your rental and strategy with your investment.

A few realities of rentvesting:

- You may forgo first-home buyer grants and stamp duty concessions on your first purchase if it's an investment rather than an owner-occupied home.
- You might be able to rent a property for far less than it would cost you to own it. The landlord is effectively subsidising your lifestyle, while you own an investment elsewhere that stacks up better as an asset.
- You need to be comfortable with the idea that your name isn't on the letterbox of the place you live in. For some people this is totally fine. For others, it feels wrong. There's no moral right or wrong here; it's just about what suits you.

Ask a mortgage broker to run scenarios both ways. Compare buying a home to live in using available grants versus rentvesting and buying an investment property elsewhere. Then ask your accountant to model the after-tax position of each scenario. It's common for people to change their mind once they see real numbers instead of assumptions.

Claire and James were renting in Brisbane and loved the city lifestyle. Long term, they wanted to build a home in a growing regional area and eventually live there when they were ready to settle down. Their worry was that if they waited too long, they would be priced out of that regional market. They modelled two scenarios with their broker and accountant.

- *Scenario 1:* They buy the regional property as an investment from day one. Because there were no first-home-buyer incentives for an investment purchase, the deposit required was significantly higher. The numbers only really worked if one of their parents provided a guarantee, which would allow them to keep renting in the city while the regional property was tenanted.
- *Scenario 2:* They build and move into the regional property as owner-occupiers for at least 12 months, which meant they could access a stamp duty concession and the $30 000 first-home-buyer grant that was available for new homes at the time. After living there for a year, they could move back to the city, rent again and turn the regional home into an investment property for the next five to seven years.

(continued)

When the scenarios were laid out, neither set of parents was comfortable offering a guarantee. If Claire and James wanted this property, the only viable option was to move there for at least 12 months.

They made the move, built the home and lived there for just over a year. During that time, the property increased in value by close to $100 000. Then Claire was transferred to Victoria through work, so their plans changed again. They moved, rented in Melbourne and the regional home became an investment that they now hold as rentvesters. They're currently considering using the equity in that property to help fund a second purchase.

o o o

Chloe and Rebecca lived on the Gold Coast and rented a home with another couple. They genuinely enjoyed their living arrangement and didn't want to change it just for the sake of owning a home. They also felt that the type of property they could afford to buy in their preferred suburbs would not perform as well as a different asset type in a different location. They had a solid deposit, but their borrowing capacity limited them. Their broker preapproved them for $550 000, but that assumed a certain rent return on the property.

After looking at various options, they decided to buy a townhouse in a strong regional centre in Queensland, where the numbers stacked up better in terms of yield and likely demand. The rent

(continued)

comfortably supported the loan, the vacancy rates had been consistently low for years and the area had multiple industries supporting local employment.

They kept renting on the Gold Coast, enjoyed their lifestyle and friendship household and let the regional townhouse quietly work in the background. For them, rentvesting was a deliberate wealth strategy, not a last resort.

Cameron rentvested through much of his 20s. On a single income, he couldn't afford to buy where he wanted to live, so he rented a small unit in an area he loved and focused his investing dollars on properties in locations where the numbers stacked up. His non-negotiable was buying house and land—that is, not a unit or townhouse. His preference was blocks that had potential for future use, such as dual access for a granny flat or the option for a future subdivision, subject to advice and approvals.

The property market today is different and that exact journey would be harder to replicate now. Cameron's story isn't necessarily the blueprint, but some principles still apply. Rentvesting, combined with sensible investing elsewhere, is one of the strategies Australians are using to build wealth when traditional owner-occupier pathways feel out of reach.

Being an ethical landlord

It's easy to joke about landlords as villains, but you don't have to be that person. You can pursue your financial goals and still treat tenants like human beings. Here are some practical ideas for being an ethical landlord.

- *Keeping rental practices fair*
  Commit from the start to not squeezing every last dollar out of your tenants. Charge a fair market rent, respond to maintenance requests promptly and don't view tenants as 'the enemy'. Most renters are simply people trying to live their lives.

- *Providing housing where it's needed*
  You might deliberately choose locations where there's genuine demand for rental housing, such as areas near hospitals, universities or major employment hubs. Some investors like the idea of owning homes that will likely house nurses, teachers or other essential workers.

- *Maintaining your property well*
  If you wouldn't live in filth, don't expect your tenants to. Keep the property in good repair. Fix things that are your responsibility. Schedule periodic upgrades when needed.

- *Considering sustainable upgrades where possible*
  If the numbers allow, adding things like solar panels, improved insulation or efficient heating and cooling can reduce bills for tenants and improve the overall appeal of the property.

- *Making small gestures*
  Small gestures, such as sending a simple Christmas card or a modest gift voucher to tenants, can also go a long way in building goodwill, but the main thing is simple: respect.

It's good to care about people. It's also okay to remember that you're running a business. You're allowed to make a profit. You're allowed to say no to situations that place you under unreasonable financial strain. The goal is to find a healthy balance between ethics and sustainability.

Freevesting: Investing while living at home

'Freevesting' is a term sometimes used to describe a strategy where you invest in property while living at home with parents or other family and paying low or no rent. Decades ago, many people left home at 18 or 19 and never came back. Today, with higher housing costs and longer periods of study, it's increasingly common for adults in their 20s and even early 30s to live at home for longer. That can feel awkward at times, but it can also create a powerful financial opportunity if it's handled intentionally.

Freevesting might look like this:

- You live at home and pay little or no board.
- You use the money you would have spent on rent to save a deposit quickly.
- You buy an investment property and keep living at home while tenants pay rent into your offset account.
- Over time, you build equity and potentially repeat the process.

For parents who are 'cash poor' but want to help their children into the market, allowing them to live at home cheaply for a period can be a very real form of support. Instead of gifting $50 000 towards a deposit, a parent might effectively gift the same value by not charging rent for two to three years, on the condition that the adult child is actually investing and not just buying more gadgets and takeaway.

Freevesting isn't for everyone. Some people need to move out for their own growth or sanity. Family dynamics can make it impractical. But if you have a healthy family setup, clear expectations and a serious commitment to investing, freevesting can accelerate your property journey significantly.

Property in action

Take a moment, make a mental note or write down / make a note in your phone: Which investing strategy feels right for you? Do you have any further questions to explore? Think through the practicalities we've discussed and your potential strategy, and choose an option to explore further with your trusted professionals.

Food for thought

Despite what your well-meaning, risk-averse relatives—who want you to buy a home to live in—might say, buying your first property as an investment isn't the second-best option. For many people it's the most realistic and powerful way to get started. It lets you:

- keep living where you want, for now
- own an asset in a location that makes sense on the numbers
- build equity and experience as a property owner
- potentially leverage into future properties, including a home to live in
- purchase in a higher growth area.

It also comes with extra responsibilities and moving parts. You need to do your research, build a strong team and be honest with yourself about your risk tolerance and your capacity to handle the occasional curveball. If you can accept that your first property doesn't have to be your forever home and that you may be better off buying a boring, sensible investment in a suburb you rarely visit, you open up a very different set of possibilities for your financial future.

The goal isn't to collect properties for the sake of it. The goal is to build a life that aligns with your values, gives you options and allows you to sleep at night. For some, that will mean living in their first home as soon as possible. For others, it will mean buying as an investment property first, rentvesting or freevesting for a season and then stepping into an owner-occupied home later.

There's no one right path; there's just the path that fits your reality, your 'why', your numbers and your version of a good life. Let's aim for that!

Start with this…

If investing is starting to feel like the right way forward, have a think about the following:

- What would be your strategy? Long-term capital growth, cash flow, tax benefits or a stepping stone for your next purchase?
- What kind of rentvesting scenario would you be interested in exploring?

7

Choosing your asset type

It sounds weird saying 'asset type' when you're buying your home. But even when you're buying a home to live in you're investing in a big asset and what you buy matters and can have some major impacts on your financial position over time.

For most of us, our family home is the largest asset we ever own. Taking some time to understand not just where you want to live, but what kind of asset you're buying, can make a meaningful difference to your long-term wealth and flexibility.

Different property types offer different levels of affordability, maintenance, growth potential, lifestyle fit, legal responsibility and also borrowing parameters. Understanding these differences is essential before you begin your search.

Even if you never plan to treat your home as an investment, it is still worth looking at it through an 'asset lens'. After all, you're borrowing a large sum of money, paying interest for years and locking your finances into this property. Understanding exactly what you're buying helps you make informed decisions now and in the future.

By the end of this chapter we hope you can compare properties and decide which type aligns to your needs.

What 'asset type' really means

Property types come with a variety of considerations, including:

- *affordability:* apartments may be cheaper than houses, but land size, strata fees and location can affect long-term costs
- *maintenance:* apartments may have more fees (such as strata or body corporate fees)
- *growth potential:* some property types may appreciate in value more quickly depending on demand, land content and location
- *lifestyle fit:* consider space, privacy, proximity to amenities and suitability for your current and future needs
- *legal and lending considerations:* some property types or zoning classifications can limit borrowing, impact loan approval or restrict what you can do with the property in the future.

How asset type impacts loan approval

Your loan approval isn't just about income and deposit; it's also about the property you're purchasing. Lenders have guidelines that vary on:

- *property type:* free-standing houses, apartments and off-the-plan purchases may have different criteria. You might have a loan approval for a 95 per cent lend but then choose a property that is a 40-square-metre unit and find out that the maximum lend as a percentage for that unit type is 80 per cent
- *zoning and title:* some land titles or zoning restrictions can limit borrowing. A property with rural or commercial zoning will be viewed differently from a residentially zoned property
- *location category:* lenders classify locations differently, which affects maximum LVR and approval conditions.

Even if you have a large deposit for your property and some of these factors don't impact your ability to borrow for the property, understanding these lending restrictions is important. It affects your ability to sell, refinance or leverage the equity in the property later.

Location

Location remains the most important factor in property, regardless of whether you're choosing a property to live in or to invest in. You can change a house. You can renovate, extend, update flooring or put a new kitchen in when budget allows but you can't change:

- the neighbourhood surrounding you
- the commute time to work
- the local schools
- the overall desirability of the area.

The old saying 'buy the worst house on the best street' comes from this.

Location also matters from a borrowing perspective. Banks and lenders often assign a category to each area based on infrastructure, demand, and growth potential.

For example:

- *Categories 1–3:* major city; well-established suburbs — maximum LVR may be up to 95 per cent
- *Category 4:* secondary regional town — LVR may be 90 per cent
- *Category 5:* remote or small town — LVR may be 80 per cent.

These classifications differ among lenders, so if you're looking at a specific postcode, it's wise to check with your broker before committing. Sometimes the location may mean you need to adjust your loan structure, your lender or your expectations about what you can borrow.

In 2023, a potential client approached Rach seeking finance to purchase a residential property they intended to live in. However, the property was zoned as 'holiday accommodation', which restricts occupancy to no more than 12 consecutive weeks at a time.

The pre-approval they had in place was for owner-occupied borrowing and did not support this zoning type. They were advised that, even if finance could be obtained, living in the property long term would breach local council regulations. Rach recommended considering alternative properties that complied with both borrowing policy and council requirements. Despite this advice, the client was determined to proceed and ultimately secured a loan directly with a lender that did not require a valuation at the time of approval.

Recently, the client returned, seeking to access the equity in the property, which has increased significantly in value. However, their current lender required a valuation and wouldn't accept the property due to its zoning. This prevented them from refinancing or leveraging the equity.

The property was then listed for sale. While there was some buyer interest, the same zoning restrictions have caused multiple prospective buyers to withdraw, impacting the client's ability to sell.

This case highlights an important lesson: it's worth pausing to consider the long-term implications of the asset being purchased—particularly how zoning and security type can affect future borrowing, refinancing and resale options.

Lifestyle and long-term flexibility

Thinking about your property as an asset doesn't mean you have to sacrifice lifestyle. But it does mean considering:

- *future family needs*: Will a one-bedroom unit work if you have children?
- *potential resale*: Is the property appealing to future buyers if you need to sell?
- *cost of ownership*: Think beyond the mortgage to maintenance, insurance, council rates and strata fees.

Even if you're buying a property purely to live in, considering these aspects upfront ensures your home remains a positive, manageable asset rather than a financial burden.

By the end of this chapter we'd like you to be able to:

- understand that every home is an asset, even if it's your first family home
- compare properties not just on style, bedrooms and price, but on long-term financial, lifestyle and lending implications
- consider how the type and location of a property aligns with your goals now and in the future.

Considering these sorts of things early on will help you make a purchase that suits both your life today and your financial future.

Unit or house?

When choosing between a unit or a house as your first property, it's important to understand how each type performs as an asset. Houses generally offer more land, which is what tends to grow in value over time, so they often have stronger long-term capital growth. They also give you more freedom to renovate or extend. However, houses usually cost more to buy and maintain. Units, on the other hand, are often more affordable and can be easier to rent out, especially in popular urban areas. But units come with strata fees, shared walls and less control over the building and they usually have slower capital growth because you're buying less land. The right choice depends on your budget, the suburb you're buying in and whether your goal is affordability, lifestyle or long-term growth.

A dilemma many first-home buyers face is choosing between lifestyle and asset type. Should you buy a unit in the city you live in, a townhouse 20 minutes out of town or a house with an hour-long commute?

The answer will always come down to what's important to you. Some questions to ask are:

- Do I value lifestyle or long-term capital growth more right now?
- Am I willing to trade space for location, or location for space?
- How important is commuting time or proximity to friends, family and work?
- Can I comfortably maintain a house, or would a low-maintenance unit suit me better?
- How do strata fees compare with the cost of maintaining a house in the areas I'm considering?
- If I bought further out, would I still be happy living there in three to five years?
- Am I choosing this property for my life today, or for the investment fundamentals long-term?
- Would a different suburb or property type help me enter the market sooner?

Ultimately, there's no 'right' answer, only the property that best aligns with your priorities, budget and long-term plans. By understanding how each asset type performs and asking yourself the right questions, you can choose a first property that truly supports your goals, both now and in the years ahead.

Back in 2015, Rach had a client who was renting a unit about 25 minutes from Sydney's CBD. They decided to buy a similar unit in the same area for about $680 000. They didn't really consider the asset type: they did what a lot of first-home buyers do and looked at what it cost to buy near where they lived, then bought what they could afford in that area.

At the time, they could have bought a house about seven minutes further from the city for roughly the same price.

Fast-forward 10 years to 2025: their unit is now worth around $705 000, which is hardly any growth in a decade. The house they could have bought would be worth over $1 000 000 today. Even though the unit suited their lifestyle, it turned out to be a weaker investment.

This doesn't mean you should always buy a house or ignore your lifestyle. It simply shows how important it is to understand property types, land value, location and market trends before you choose what to buy. Make sure you look at how values in the area have moved over time so you can make an informed decision, not just one based on how the property feels today.

New builds vs older properties

One of the most common dilemmas we hear of people buying properties is around buying a new vs older property: 'Should I buy a newer home further from where I work or an older home closer in?' If you're buying a property to live in, it will always come down to your personal preference. But if you're thinking about capital growth and long-term investment potential, here are a few things to consider.

The pros of new builds:

- *Renovation:* minimal renovation is required in the early years
- *Scarcity:* new developments in certain areas can be limited, creating demand
- *Gentrified location:* some new homes are part of up-and-coming suburbs, which can support future growth
- *Land size:* land parcels in new estates may be larger
- *Future growth:* modern infrastructure and planned developments around the area can enhance property values.

The cons of new builds:

- Higher purchase prices relative to older homes in the same suburb
- Smaller yards in some estates, especially in inner or high-demand locations
- Less character compared with established homes; finishes can be basic in mass-built estates
- Limited rental history for investors to benchmark yield or growth potential.

The pros of older properties:

- *Established suburbs:* often closer to work, schools, transport and amenities
- *Character and charm:* architectural features, higher ceilings, larger gardens

- *Potential to add value:* opportunity for renovations, extensions, or landscaping to increase capital growth
- *Land size:* older homes sometimes sit on larger blocks than new builds in the same area
- *Immediate community:* established neighbourhoods with known demographics and services.

The cons of older properties:

- *Maintenance costs:* roofs, plumbing, wiring and other features may need updating
- *Energy efficiency:* older homes may lack modern insulation, windows or solar options
- *Renovation requirements:* to achieve long-term growth or personal preference, renovation may be necessary
- *Zoning and planning limits:* extensions or rebuilds may be restricted by council regulations.

Choosing between a new or older property will always come down to balancing your lifestyle preferences, budget and long-term plans. Consider what's more important to you: convenience, character and potential to add value, or certainty, modern finishes and minimal upkeep. Running the numbers and understanding growth potential in the area can help guide your decision.

Title types

When we talk about properties we usually say house, townhouse or unit; however, there's another element to a property and that's the title type. Both the asset type and title type are important to understand because they explain what you're actually buying. But they also affect things like what you may be able to do with the property and can impact your borrowing.

You may have a pre-approval for a unit: most of these are strata titles. If you were looking at a company title unit, you'd need to check with your broker that this fits your approval. The contract of sale will have the title type on the front page and it's also generally stated in the real estate listing.

Understanding the title type upfront ensures you know exactly what you're buying, helps you avoid surprises with lenders or insurers, and clarifies your responsibilities and flexibility with the property.

Title types impact the asset you're buying. They show how the property is managed — that is, by an owners corporation (this varies by state — you may have heard terms like 'body corporate', 'strata' or 'community association') — and can also impact your finance. Your lender will give a pre-approval assuming a standard property. So if you're buying a strata unit (and there will be strata fees) the lender needs to know. If it is, say, a company title rather than a strata title, it may impact how much you can borrow.

For example, many lenders won't lend to a company title property with the same LVR as a strata title, so it matters to find this out and let your broker know the title type you are looking at. Even if it does not impact your borrowing, it may affect the finance options for a potential buyer if you sell, so you need to know if there are any restrictions and how they may impact you.

When you look at the contract of sale, it will tell you the title type, usually on the front page under 'folio identifier'. Working closely with your conveyancer and mortgage broker is really important when checking these details.

Let's unpack the types of titles you will find during your property search.

Freehold land (Torrens Title)

With freehold land (Torrens Title), you own both the land and the building on it. It will usually be a house though some townhouses may also be Torrens title (or they might be community or strata title). This is the most common title type and is often considered the gold standard of home ownership. You have full freedom in decision making, you can manage your own maintenance and you can enjoy clear, guaranteed ownership.

Strata title

Buying a strata unit (whether it's an apartment, townhouse or villa) can be a great way to enter the property market, especially in areas where houses are too expensive. Or maybe you simply love unit living and all of the conveniences it offers. A strata unit is a property within a larger building or development where you own your 'lot' (your individual apartment or townhouse) and share ownership of common property, such as hallways, gardens, driveways and shared facilities like gyms, pools or BBQ areas. Strata units are governed by by-laws, which might restrict pets, noise levels, flooring types or how you use your balcony. In recent times, committees around Australia have made by-laws (after a vote to lot owners) stating that properties can't be used for short-term letting of fewer than three days (to avoid disruption on the property from Airbnb-type stays). Decisions can be made if the committee for the property agree. You will pay strata levies (also known as body corporate or owners corporation fees) to maintain common areas and usually need permission from the owners corporation for major renovations or changes to the exterior of your property.

> The word *strata* comes from Latin and means 'layers'.
>
> Geologists use it to describe layers of rock. Property law borrowed the same idea to explain layered ownership in buildings such as apartments and townhouses. New South Wales introduced the world's first strata title system in 1961, and the model spread across Australia and beyond.

If you're considering purchasing a strata unit, it's important to understand the responsibilities involved:

- You will pay quarterly strata levies, which cover maintenance, administration and a capital works fund (previously called a sinking fund).
- You will have to comply with by-laws, including rules around pets, renovations and noise.
- You should consider participating in owners' meetings and to vote to ensure your perspective is heard and considered alongside other owners. This isn't compulsory, but then don't be upset if something is agreed on and you didn't attend and vote at a meeting.

A good strata assessment carried out with your conveyancer should include:

- *the property's financial position*. Check the balance of the admin and capital works funds. Low balances or frequent special levies can signal potential issues
- *the building's condition*. Look for maintenance issues such as roof problems, concrete cancer, waterproofing or cladding concerns

- *reading through meeting minutes.* Review recent AGM and committee minutes for disputes, noise complaints or costly repairs
- *checking insurance details.* Ensure the building insurance is current and adequate
- *considering the number of units.* Larger complexes can bring more personalities and potential conflicts within the committee
- *checking out the facilities.* Gyms, lifts, gardens and pools increase ongoing costs
- *delving into the strata management.* Is it professionally managed? Minutes should indicate whether the committee is organised and proactive
- *looking out for special levies.* Be aware of one-off payments, usually required when the committee hasn't saved enough for major repairs.

Another key consideration is unit size, which can impact both finance approval and resale. Some lenders have restrictions, such as:

- not lending to studios
- minimum internal floor space requirements (e.g. 40 m^2)
- restrictions on certain unit sizes in specific postcodes deemed high risk.

If you're looking at a certain type of property, such as studios in a particular postcode, make sure your broker knows so they can check lender requirements. Even if you're pre-approved, it's important to check whether what you're buying could have restrictions for future buyers.

Community title

Similarly to strata title, community title applies to developments with shared facilities and common areas, but it often includes a wider range of property types, such as detached houses within a larger community (e.g. a gated community). Owners have individual titles for their properties and share ownership of the common areas and facilities, which are managed by a community association.

Company title

This involves you buying shares in a company that owns the building. Your shareholding gives you the right to occupy a specific unit and voting rights. Company title is different from strata title because the company owns the building and you buy shares in that company. Some lenders restrict lending on company title properties and some don't lend to them at all.

Leasehold title

You'll find this mainly in the ACT. Under this system, the land is not sold to an individual. Instead, the right to occupy and use the land is leased for a specific period, often several decades (up to 99 years).

Zoning

Unlike title type, which relates to proof of ownership and rights (freehold, leasehold, community, strata, company), zoning controls how the land can be used (planning laws). The zoning can affect how much a bank will lend, especially for properties with non-standard zoning.

In most cases you'll be looking at a standard zoning. In New South Wales this is R1 General Residential; in Victoria it is called Neighbourhood Residential Zone (NRZ); and in Queensland it's known as General Residential Zone, to give some examples.

Zoning shows what the land can be used for and any restrictions that may apply. It's important to understand this before you start looking at properties because anything other than standard zoning (for example, commercial, rural or environmental) may affect your ability to get finance.

There are many different zones across all states — too many to go through in detail here. The key takeaway is to always check the zoning before getting too serious about a property and if it's anything other than standard residential, run it past your broker first.

Here are some examples of where finance might be an issue:

- You're pre-approved for a standard property; however, you choose a 100-acre property that's rurally zoned. Two things you need to check with your broker are whether your lender will lend to 100 acres (size) and whether they will take a rurally zoned property.

- You find a property that has holiday zoning. This is popular in Victoria and New South Wales and has rules about how long you can stay there. The agent says it's fine because so many people stay there full time; however, the bank or lender may not lend to this zoning at all, or at a much reduced LVR.

- You find a property that has residential zoning; however, there's a commercial lease in place. The commercial lease impacts your ability to borrow, even though the zoning is residential.

- You're approved for a 20-acre property and zoning of 1A Rural; however, the property you find is currently being used as a working farm. The zoning is fine but the usage of the property may impact your loan approval, even if your zoning is accepted.

Property in action

Pick a property you're interested in and find out as much as you can about it. What type of title does it have? What is the zoning? Practise assessing these details and think about how they could affect your purchase and borrowing.

House-and-land packages

When you start looking at homes, you'll quickly come across the term 'house-and-land package'. It sounds straightforward, but there's more to it than just buying a block of land with a house on it. These packages are popular because you get a brand-new home, and state-based government incentives can make them one of the most affordable entry point by reducing the deposit required when grants are higher for new homes. They're especially attractive offers for first-time property buyers!

What is a house-and-land package?

A house-and-land package is essentially a deal where you buy a block of land and then contract a builder to construct a home on that land. While it's marked 'package', the purchase usually happens in two parts:

1. *The land purchase*: you buy a block of land from a developer.

2. *The building contract*: you enter into an agreement with a builder to construct your home on that land.

Sometimes these are bundled together by a developer for ease of marketing and sale (showing you what they look like and cost together), but legally and financially they remain separate contracts: one for the land, then one for the build.

Something to note here is settlement dates and your pre-approval. If you are buying a block of land from the developer, when is it expected to settle? If it's in a year's time and your pre-approval only lasts three months, how does this work? You'll need to be confident your loan will be approved again at the time, so there is always an element of risk here.

Types of house-and-land packages

There are a couple of house-and-land package types to be aware of.

TURNKEY PACKAGES

This is a fully completed home, ready to move into once construction is finished. Everything is included down to the driveway, landscaping, flooring and even the letterbox. These packages are hassle-free. They're possibly more expensive upfront, but there's nothing more to add. They're popular for investors who wish to move a tenant straight in and don't want to be involved with minor selections.

STANDARD HOUSE-AND-LAND PACKAGES

These are the most common types you will see in the market. They're often advertised with a 'base price' to look appealing but may not include things deemed essential by you — or by the bank for finance — such as fencing, flooring, air conditioning, window coverings or a driveway. If you're buying a standard house-and-land package as a first-home buyer, do your research. Know and understand your contract and be clear about what's included and what's not.

Work alongside your mortgage broker throughout this process because you shouldn't sign anything until you fully understand what's included and what's required for finance. You may think, 'Oh, my mate Dave is a concreter; he can put the driveway in later when I've saved more money', but your bank may not agree to finance the home because they may deem a completed driveway as essential for completion.

Rach would say the most regrets and misunderstandings she has seen from clients over her career involve house-and-land packages—not because they're a bad idea, but because buyers commit or pay a deposit before fully understanding the process and how every step works.

> One piece of advice: don't use the builder's finance person. Use someone independent who truly understands all facets of the contract for both land and build. Ensure you know what's involved before signing anything. We know what it feels like sitting in that room with the salesperson pressuring you to sign today 'or the price will go up' … this is a sales tactic you should never fall for. Sign when you fully understand and feel empowered.

Common traps and pitfalls and how to avoid them

Seeing the display home and believing that's what you get is a big trap. The display home has the top-of-the-line finishes and inclusions. Walk through the house with a pen and paper and ask the salesperson, 'Are these the tiles I will be getting?' and 'Is this the number of power points included in my contract?' Every single detail matters so over-ask and over-confirm to ensure you know exactly what's included in the price.

Paying funds before 'colour selections' is another trap. Colour selections aren't just about colour; they include electrical fittings, floor coverings, light fittings, tiles, kitchen benches and splashbacks. If you have a figure in mind that you can afford, make sure all of these items are included in that number before signing. Rach can't count the number of clients who were forced to borrow from family because they didn't realise there would be an extra $50 000 needed to complete the house!

Beware of giveaways; they come at a cost. A sale advertising 'free wine fridge and $60 000 of extras' sounds great, but don't let it take your eye off the essentials you need to finance your home, like carpet and tiles. Beware the shiny objects!

Landscaping often isn't included. That's fine, but look carefully at your block and contract. Many people think, 'Landscaping isn't included, but I can put lawns and plants in later', only to find they need $40 000 for an essential retaining wall or outdoor drainage, both of which fall under 'landscaping'.

> Ask this question when walking through the display home: 'You quoted $X as a base price for this house. How much would it cost to build exactly what we are standing in, turn-key, everything included?' This will reveal the difference and how quickly costs add up. Rach has often had first-home buyers say to her, 'The builder said $X, but after asking for everything needed for the bank to fund the loan, it's 50 per cent more'.
>
> Please don't let this put you off going down this path, but take it as a fair warning: be informed and go into that display village like a pro. Rach personally paid someone (about $700) to review her build contract (also called a tender) before signing—and she's in the game!

The house-and-land buying process

Here's a run-down of the steps in the house-and-land buying process.

1. *Choose your block of land*: usually in a new estate or subdivision; developers release stages in growth areas

2. *Select a house design*: builders have a range of standard designs you can choose from, often with multiple options like a choice of façade (the front of the house) and alfresco area

3. *Sign two contracts*: one for the land and one for the build. Find out things like how long it will take, whether the land is ready now and whether you'll need to wait for council approval. These can take years to finalise and you need to be informed before you sign. Can you afford to wait? Work this out and ask a lot of questions.

4. *Settle on the land*: this might be straight away, or it may be when the land is 'registered', which could be a year after you paid a deposit. Remember that finance pre-approval is valid for three months so you'll need to have your loan approved again if the land settles later than that. This is usually fine but not if your situation has changed (e.g. you're now on parental leave or have changed from employee to self-employed).

5. *Make progress payments for the build* (also known as a construction loan): we addressed this in chapter 3, but essentially this is drawn down in stages and you only pay interest on what's owing at each stage of the build. Note that you only pay stamp duty on the land, not the build (this is a great saving) *but* you must pay interest on the land at the stages of the construction loan until you're finished. Are you prepared for this? Do you have funds to cover rent and progressive payments over the build time? How long is the build going to take? Are you prepared for delays and can you cover the interest for that period of time?

Key risks with house-and-land packages

Before you sign on the dotted line, there are a few risks to be aware of with house-and-land packages

The timing risk:

- Land might not be registered when you sign
- Registration delays can be months or years
- Construction start depends on land settlement
- Build time frames often blow out due to labour, weather or supply issues
- Finance approvals expire and must be re-approved at settlement
- Life changes during delays can derail lending
    - Parental leave
    - Job change
    - Moving to self-employed

You need patience and flexibility to handle delays without your plan falling over.

The cash-flow risk:

- You pay interest during construction before moving in
- You may be paying rent and loan interest at the same time
- Progress payments increase gradually as the build advances

- Delays extend how long you're paying interest without living there
- Final costs can increase due to variations and upgrades
- You must have cash buffers, not just borrowing power.

House-and-land builds reward planning and punish tight cash flow. There are two things to note:

1. *Valuation matters.* When you buy land that won't be registered for a while, the bank will value it again at settlement and lend based on that number. If the valuation is higher, great. But if it comes in lower, the bank may lend less and you'll need to cover the gap. This can be a real issue if you're borrowing at 95 per cent because even a small drop in value can mean finding extra cash or risking the deposit you've already paid.
2. *If you're using a big government incentive to fund your deposit, check when it's paid.* There have been many cases where first-home buyers had to borrow money from family to put towards the deposit for the land because a 10 per cent deposit was required. They would only have saved 5 per cent, not realising that the government's 5 per cent wouldn't become available until the build phase. That's fine if you can borrow money, but what if you can't? Find out all the steps before you start and make sure you're covered at every stage.

Buying land then building

Though less common for first-home buyers, buying a block of land and then building gives you complete freedom. You can choose any block you like, buy it, then choose a builder and a home design to suit that land. It's less common because there's more uncertainty and more variables. In a house-and-land package, you're generally buying a block in an estate that's flat or needs minimal work to get building ready. But if you choose land in an established area, it may be sloped, rocky or have trees that need to be removed, all of which adds cost and won't be included in your builder's contract. You may also need more funds upfront.

The process is similar: you buy the land, then build on it. But you need a builder to quote on not just the house but also the cost of building on that specific block. Site costs can run into the hundreds of thousands, so you need to understand the full project before committing. Many buyers have purchased land without fully understanding how much it would cost to put a home on that block.

Some things to consider:

- *BAL rating*: this is the Bushfire Attack Level. Bushfire ratings can increase build costs depending on the level.
- *Slope*: the flatter the block, the cheaper it is to build. Always get a site cost estimate from your builder before buying land.
- *Soil testing*: builders may need to test the soil before they can give an accurate quote.
- *Clearing*: removing trees or vegetation can be expensive (you might not know what's underneath!).
- *Services and connections*: check which utilities are connected and what you'll need to organise.
- *Flood zones*: land near water may require elevated builds or extra engineering.

- *Access and setbacks*: consider how easily trades can access the block and whether this adds cost.
- *Insurance costs*: if you're near a bush fire zone, flooding area or a place prone to cyclones your home insurance will be higher. Don't forget this in the excitement of building a new home.

If you're borrowing for the build, the bank might only fund the build contract itself. You might need your own funds to cover anything outside the contract.

> The biggest out-of-contract cost Rach has seen was $200 000. Her client had bought a stunning 12-acre block of land just 10 minutes out of town for $1.2 million with a $1 million build contract. They'd budgeted the 20 per cent deposits and were funding 80 per cent of both the land and the build. Everything seemed perfect.
>
> Then the builder started clearing the site and hit rock. Lots of it. Not budgeted. Not optional. Suddenly, an extra $200 000 was needed. And here's the kicker: the bank valuation didn't increase. The client had to find that money themselves.
>
> It's an extreme case, but it shows exactly what can happen.

Before you buy land — whether a house-and-land package or a block to build on — remember, you're not just buying dirt. You're buying slope, soil, sunlight, restrictions and risk. A little extra due diligence before signing could save you a lot of heartache (and a small fortune).

Buying off the plan

Buying a property off the plan—that is, purchasing before it's built or completed—can have some advantages, but it also comes with particular risks. Understanding how off-the-plan purchases work will help you decide whether this path aligns with your goals and, most importantly, your risk tolerance.

First, what does 'off the plan' mean? It refers to buying a home or apartment based on plans, before the construction has finished or in some cases, even started. You commit to the purchase via a contract, pay a deposit and then wait until the building is completed.

This approach allows you to secure a property at today's prices. Other benefits include:

- *potential capital growth before settlement*: you could see value increase before you even move in, giving you instant equity
- *government incentives*: off-the-plan properties generally qualify for new-build first-home-buyer grants and may also attract additional stamp duty concessions
- *lower maintenance costs*: everything is brand new, so repairs and maintenance are minimal in the early years.

Sounds great, right? But for first-home buyers, off-the-plan purchases can be risky due to the uncertainty involved. Completion delays, changes to the final product or market fluctuations before settlement can all impact the outcome, so careful consideration and advice is essential before committing.

In addition, the same risks can and do apply with off-the-plan purchases as with house-and-land packages.

A general rule of thumb for any new builds or off-the-plan purchases is that whatever time frame you are given by a sales team or builder, expect that it will be extended by as much as more than a year.

Off-the-plan: a practical checklist for first-home buyers:

- ☑ *Understand the contract*: know exactly what you're signing up for, including completion dates, deposit requirements and penalties for delays or changes.
- ☑ *Check developer reputation*: research the developer's track record for delivering projects on time and to specification.
- ☑ *Assess the plans carefully*: look at floorplans, finishes and inclusions. Ask what might change before completion.
- ☑ *Consider finance timing*: your loan may only be drawn at settlement, so ensure you can meet the deposit and any interim costs.
- ☑ *Investigate market trends*: off-the-plan properties are bought at today's price, but market values can rise or fall before settlement.
- ☑ *Understand government incentives*: confirm which grants or stamp duty concessions apply and their timing.
- ☑ *Ask about ongoing fees*: even though it's new, consider body corporate or strata fees and any future levies.

Established properties

One of the most common purchases for first-home buyers is an already built home on a block of land in the area they live. Sounds simple! The advantage is certainty: you can see exactly what you're buying, including the home, the land and the overall layout. You also know the condition of the property, what maintenance might be needed and how it fits with the neighbourhood. While it may not have the 'brand-new' appeal or government incentives of a new build, an established home can offer a clear picture of costs, lifestyle and location, which is often exactly what first-home buyers need. Just ensure you get a pest and building inspection to prevent buying a termite-fest!

Properties with value-add potential

When most first-home buyers think about value they think about growth and buying in the right suburb and hope time does the rest. But another way value can be created is through what the property can do, not just where it is.

Some properties offer opportunities to add value in the future, whether that's through subdivision, adding a second dwelling or building a granny flat—or even simply having enough land to extend the property down the track. Even if you never plan to do these things, understanding whether the option exists can be incredibly powerful. A good saying is, 'never turn down an option'.

But let us be clear: this is not encouraging first-home buyers to become developers. This is about buying flexibility.

You may never subdivide, you may never add a second dwelling or build a granny flat, but the next buyer might. Properties with future potential tend to:

- appeal to a broader buyer pool
- hold value better in softer markets
- offer options if your financial or family situation changes
- create pathways to income without selling.

In property, optionality is valuable.

Common ways to add value

Here are some common ways property buyers consider to add value to what they've purchased.

SUBDIVISION POTENTIAL

Some blocks can be legally subdivided based on zoning, lot size, frontage and council rules. For a first-home buyer, this doesn't mean you need to subdivide, it simply means the land itself may hold additional long-term value.

SECOND DWELLING POTENTIAL

Some properties allow for a second dwelling, often those on larger or corner sites. This can create flexibility, whether for family accommodation or rental income.

GRANNY-FLAT POTENTIAL

In many states, granny flats can be approved under simplified planning rules. They can provide additional income or housing for families, but they are not suitable for every lifestyle or budget.

Potential only matters if it is:

* legally permissible
* financially viable
* suitable for your lifestyle.

ooo

First-home buyers shouldn't overpay based on assumptions about future development. Always confirm zoning, council restrictions and lender appetite.

Value-add potential isn't for everyone but in order to understand asset types it's important to be aware of this. Understanding a property's potential helps ensure you buy what works for you long term, even if your plans change.

Jemima was a client of Rach's who had listened to the podcast. She bought her first home in 2021 and lived in it. By 2024 she was ready to use the equity she had built in property 1 to buy property 2. She was only looking at properties with potential value-add as her goal was to use the equity in both of these properties to buy her owner occupied in 2026. She purchased a three-bedroom home on a large block. In late 2025 it was valued at $200 000 more than when she purchased it in 2024. The market as a whole in the area had not risen that much but what had risen was the number of investors in the market in late 2025 looking for similar properties. When investors came heavily into the market in the cycle so did the potential for a future granny flat or for subdivision.

Jemima had no plans to sell or to build a granny flat at that time; however, the equity in her valuation in late 2025 supported her goal of buying her owner-occupied property in 2026. The asset type she chose in 2024 assisted her goal even though she never used the options that came with it.

Grant and Maya purchased a home in the eastern suburbs of Sydney. The value had increased incredibly since they purchased it. It was an older cottage on a large block. The home no longer served their family and they wished to sell and upsize; however, they couldn't find a home in the area in their price range.

Scenarios on a suitable mortgage had them moving suburbs away, which wouldn't have been worth the extra bedrooms to them. They didn't want to move due to school zones and their children's network.

They looked at two options: one was subdividing and selling a part of the block. At the time, council restrictions wouldn't allow that (they were set to change but it could have taken years). The second option was a knock-down rebuild; however, the mortgage they would have been left with was significant.

As their block was large, they were able to knock the home down and build two four-bedroom duplexes. They sold one of the duplexes when completed and were left with a manageable mortgage and a superior home in the area where they wished to live.

The asset type they chose initially left them with some options to look at later and those options were life changing for them. They had never planned to do this when they bought but they did know that land size would provide options down the track.

Things to consider when viewing properties

It's easy to be wowed by a beautifully styled or renovated home, but first-home buyers need to see past the staging or the beautiful renders their designers display on their website or pamphlets. Sellers who have mastered property styling or minor renovations can demand a premium because it creates an emotional hook. Educating yourself to see past these elements helps you identify the true potential of a home and avoid paying over market value.

A well-styled property can create an emotional hook, but if you're impressed by the styling rather than the home itself, you may be paying more than the market price because of these emotions. Buying a poorly presented property can have an upside: you can add value quickly with a freshen-up and minor improvements, potentially creating instant equity. Cotality notes that styling can add $20 000 to $50 000 to a home sale price, so being aware of this can help you make a more informed decision.

Tying it all in

When buying your first home, it's easy to focus on how the property looks and how it feels to live in, but it's just as important to understand what you're buying from an asset perspective. Your home is likely the largest financial commitment you'll ever make and different property types, locations, titles, zoning and levels of future potential all carry different risks, costs, lending rules and long-term outcomes. Looking at a property through an asset lens doesn't mean sacrificing lifestyle. It means making informed decisions about where you buy, what you buy, how easily it can be financed and how flexible it will be if your circumstances change. By understanding these factors upfront, you put yourself in a stronger position to choose a home that supports both your life today and your financial future.

Start with this . . .

Take some time to consider what kind of asset is right for you:

* Would an apartment, townhouse or detached house be more in line with your strategy?
* If you've been considering building a new property, have you considered the timelines, risks and how your borrowing will need to work?

8

The buying process

Buying your first home can feel like stepping into a game where everyone else already knows the rules. There's jargon flying around, big decisions to make and a lot of money on the move. But once you lay it all out from start to finish — from pre-approval to settlement — you realise it's not magic. It's just a process. And once you understand that process, you can move through it with confidence instead of second-guessing every step.

This chapter walks you through the real deal. Not the polished sales pitch from real estate agents. Not your mate's half-baked advice. And definitely not the 2 am doomscroll that leaves you more confused than when you started. This is a straight-talking, practical guide for first-home buyers. Step by step. We'll cover property cycles and the order in which things happen, whether you're buying by private treaty (fancy way to say normal process) or braving the chaos of an auction.

Let's start at the beginning.

Understanding property cycles

Over the past few years, Australia's property market has experienced an extraordinary run. Almost everyone seems to know someone who has built a 'mega portfolio' or made impressive gains from a single property. But periods of rapid growth can create a false sense of security, especially for first-home buyers who may not have seen a full property cycle before.

In fact, many people offering advice in professional roles today haven't lived through an entire cycle themselves. This makes it even more important for first-home buyers to understand how cycles work — not so you can 'time the market,' but so you can manage your debt, protect your risk and avoid making decisions based on the assumption that property values always rise.

Property cycles help you understand that markets move through phases of growth, stagnation and decline. Knowing this prepares you for the long journey of home ownership.

What is a property cycle?

A property cycle is the repeating pattern that real estate markets move through over time. It typically includes four broad phases:

1. recovery
2. boom/upswing
3. peak
4. downturn/correction.

You'll find an example in figure 8.1.

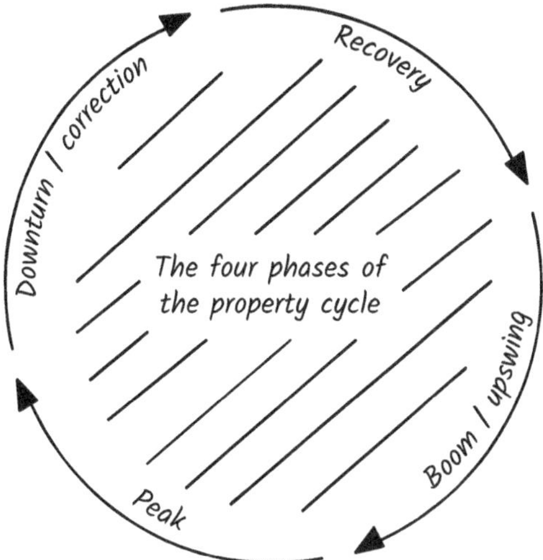

Figure 8.1: the four phases of the property cycle

While similar patterns happen in many countries, it's crucial to read *Australia-specific* information. Our market behaves differently from, say, the United States, even if global cycles often move in similar directions.

The four phases of the property cycle

Let's delve a little deeper into the four phases.

1 RECOVERY

The market begins stabilising after a decline. Confidence slowly returns, prices flatten and early signs of growth may appear.

2 BOOM / UPSWING

This is the period of strong growth. It's the one that most people notice and talk about.

Typical signs include:

- strong buyer demand
- investors returning

- media hype about the 'hot market'
- FOMO (fear-of-missing-out).

Challenges for buyers include:

- it's harder to negotiate
- properties sell quickly
- emotional decisions become more common.

This is often when inexperienced buyers stretch themselves too far.

3 PEAK

At the top of the cycle, growth slows and begins to flatten. The market becomes more unpredictable and buyers who enter at this point may be taking on higher risk.

This is also the stage when new 'creative lending solutions' start appearing, usually targeted at people desperate to buy before they 'miss out'. Loan types offered at this stage can be dangerous if the market turns shortly afterwards.

4 DOWNTURN / CORRECTION

Prices may fall or remain flat for an extended period. There are more properties on the market and sentiment shifts.

Typical signs include:

- price reductions
- fewer buyers
- properties taking longer to sell
- developers slowing construction.

This can create a *buyer's market*, with more choice and less competition. However, downturns may also come with *tighter lending conditions*, which can make borrowing more difficult even when prices look appealing.

What influences property cycles?

Property cycles don't happen randomly. They're shaped by a combination of:

- interest rates
- employment levels and wage growth
- population growth
- government incentives or policies
- construction supply
- consumer confidence.

Understanding these factors helps you recognise where the market might be heading, though not with perfect accuracy.

Why first-home buyers shouldn't stress about 'perfect timing'

No-one can predict the market with certainty, not even experts. The best time for you to buy is when:

- you're financially ready
- you feel comfortable with repayments

- you have a long-term plan
- you understand the risks of the cycle.

Many first-home buyers get caught out by assuming prices will always rise. Cycles remind us that markets move in *both* directions. Your goal isn't to buy at the lowest point; it's to make smart, long-term decisions and avoid overexposure during peak phases.

Selling in a downturn — when waiting isn't an option

Most people will assume selling in a downturn is something that happens to other people. It's easy to believe you'll always be able to wait out the market, sell when prices are strong and make decisions from a position of control. And in an ideal world, that's exactly what happens.

Over the years, Rach has seen clients who were forced to sell in a softer or declining market, not because they made bad decisions but because circumstances changed. Understanding when and why people end up selling in a downturn is important. We don't say this to scare you, but to help you plan with enough flexibility so you don't become one of them. Most forced sales have nothing to do with the property itself. They're usually driven by:

- job loss or prolonged income reduction
- relationship breakdowns
- health issues
- family responsibilities
- business failure

- over-stretching borrowing capacity
- further debt taken on after the mortgage.

The market downturn removes the buffer.

Chris and Jenny purchased their home at the peak of a strong market. With their dual incomes they felt comfortable stretching their borrowing capacity, assuming income growth would follow.

One year after buying, Jenny was made redundant. They had an emergency buffer, but it was small. Three months after redundancy Jenny still couldn't find work. With no cash reserves, they were forced to sell.

The sale occurred in a market where it wasn't ideal to sell. After agents' costs they walked away with $12 000—about $50 000 less than their initial deposit. This wasn't because they bought badly but because their structure didn't allow them to absorb income shock.

The lesson wasn't about timing; it was about buffers.

Kai and Brett purchased a home using what's commonly referred to as 'gap finance': a lender lent them 80 per cent of their purchase, they had saved 5 per cent deposit and they borrowed the other 15 per cent from another lender. The 15 per cent was at a higher rate and a shorter term than a home loan and the broker had told them that 'as prices always rise they can just refinance this part when the house value goes up'. The problem was the house didn't rise in value over the next two years and

(continued)

the repayments across the two loans became unmanageable. It was only ever meant to be a short-term solution.

Kai and Brett had to sell their home and although they left with slightly more funds than they had purchased for, as they were no longer first-home buyers they weren't able to lean on things like stamp duty concessions to buy and needed substantially more deposit to enter the market. It took them three years to save enough to re-enter the market. In retrospect, they may well have thought it would have been better to wait a bit longer to enter the market the first time rather than using a solution that can end up being quite costly.

Bree and Luke bought their first home in 2019. It was their first time living together. They were confident in their ability to service the loan and had adequate buffers in place. In 2021, during the second COVID lockdown, their relationship ended. They were based in Victoria and in their area this wasn't an ideal time to sell. Neither party could afford to service the loan alone and refinancing wasn't an option as there wasn't enough equity to access more funds. Bree and Luke sold for less than they bought the home for and ended up having to take out a personal loan to be able to sell as there was a shortfall at the end.

Property decisions don't pause for personal circumstances and markets don't wait for perfect timing.

These examples illustrate how buyers who stretch themselves during a boom, or rely on risky lending products, may be forced to sell at the wrong time, locking in losses and limiting future opportunities.

Unpacking the buying process

Let's move on and unpack the property-buying process step by step (see figure 8.2). It's important to note that the property-buying process is largely state based. This means you'll need guidance from your 'dream team' (see chapter 9) pertinent to the state you're buying in (not living in, if you're buying an investment property outside your own state).

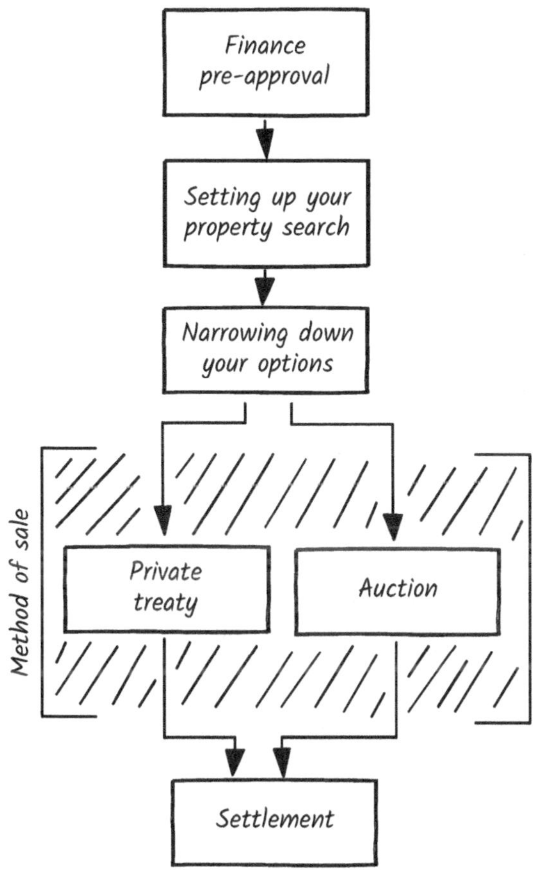

Figure 8.2: the buying process

Pre-approval: The green light to get moving

Pre-approval is the moment buying stops being a hypothetical and starts becoming real. You might have already been scrolling realestate .com.au like it's a part-time job, but until you have pre-approval, agents won't take you seriously and you can't confidently make offers. Pre-approval tells the world (and more importantly *you*) that a lender is willing to lend you a certain amount under certain conditions.

Your mortgage broker—or lender, if you're going direct—collects your documents, assesses your borrowing capacity, submits your application and a lender reviews your situation. They'll look at income, expenses, savings history, liabilities, existing debts, credit score and a whole heap of numbers that only make sense to people who love spreadsheets.

Once you're pre-approved, your broker will explain the details: your maximum purchase price, what your repayments would look like, how your loan will be structured and the conditions the lender has attached. This is incredibly important because pre-approval isn't a blank cheque; it's a framework within which you can safely shop.

It's important to note that *pre-approval* is not *formal approval*. There are conditions, so you need to check what they are. Generally, they require a suitable property and a valuation, but the bank can come back and ask for anything here. Any changes to your income or your personal situation can impact your approval so keep close to your broker and don't make changes, such as changing jobs or taking on additional debt, without checking with them first.

Setting up your property search

A good search starts not with clicking on every home in your price bracket, but with clarity. What do you need? What do you value? What fits your life today and the life you see ahead?

A typical first-home buyer search usually begins broad. You might start with a handful of suburbs based on price, commute, lifestyle or schools, depending on your stage of life. You'll compare apartments vs townhouses vs houses. You'll look at strata fees, land size, proximity to transport. It's normal to start with a big list of 'must-haves' and realise within a week that some of them aren't actually must-have, they're more 'nice if it falls into our laps'.

Setting up your search also includes the less romantic but very strategic part: understanding the market you're walking into. Are properties selling quickly? Are they selling above guide? What trends do the recent sale prices show? This is where conversations with your broker, buyers agents or even local agents can help. And yes, agents will sometimes try to 'sell the dream' a bit too hard, but they also see the patterns before most people.

Once you've defined your criteria, set your price limit and worked out your non-negotiables, it's time to inspect. A lot. The average first-home buyer in Australia inspects more than 30 properties before buying. That's not a sign you're doing something wrong — it's how your brain learns what good value looks like.

The more homes you see, the sharper your instincts become.

Narrowing down your options

After a few weeks of inspections, something interesting happens: you start recognising patterns. You walk into a home and instantly know if it's overpriced. You see through staging, you notice things you missed early on, you start asking better questions. Narrowing down your options isn't just picking your favourite — it's filtering out anything that doesn't serve your strategy. The goal here is to identify the handful of properties that genuinely fit your budget, lifestyle and long-term goals.

This is also the point where you start thinking about how each property would stack up in the real world. How would the morning light fall? Where would you put the couch? Is there enough storage? Does the layout flow?

But more importantly: what risks come with this property?

- Is it in a flood zone?
- Are the strata fees enormous?
- Is there a planned development next door?
- Does the building have a problematic history?
- Has it been on the market for too long?
- Is the vendor looking for a quick sale?
- What are comparable sales in the area telling you?

Put your feelings to one side, just for a second, and complete a comparison table of the homes you're considering. Table 8.1 is a great example. By comparing the big features and major things that can't be changed—like land size and distance to school (or beach, *wink*)—you can start to compare the big-ticket items without getting too swept away with little things like those ugly stain-glass windows on that hideous bi-fold door. You must always go back to your hard considerations (e.g. cost/budget and number of rooms), soft considerations (prefer brick and a flat yard) and deal-breakers.

By the time you're ready to make an offer, or bid at auction, you should feel informed, not intimidated.

You can download a blank spreadsheet by following the QR code on page 300 and customise it to your own needs.

Table 8.1: your property checklist and research table

	Desired	Property 1	Property 2	Property 3
Address		6/26 Station Street	4/12 James Lane	43 Spring Avenue
Agent name		Paula D	Michael M	Ken C
Sale type		Auction	Private treaty	Auction (made it clear they were open to pre-action offers)
Approx. age		20 years	2 years	35 years
List date		March	June	June
List price		\$900k–\$1.05m	\$950k	No official guide
Sale price		\$970k		
Offer made			\$930k	
Sale date		23-Apr		
If for investment				
Weekly rent				
Current tenancy and term				
Gross yield				
Hard considerations				
Budget/ purchase price	Under \$980k	Yes	Yes	Possibly around \$1m
Bedrooms	3	3	3 plus study	3
Bathrooms	2	2.5	2	2
Parking	2	1 covered 1 driveway	Double lockup	1 covered 1 driveway
Condition	Near new (within 5 years)	Old, but looked decent	Newish, 2 years	Felt tired. New kitchen within last 2 years. Bathrooms need doing.
Desired school catchments	Within	Outside	Within	Within
Soft considerations				
Type	House	Townhouse	Townhouse	House
Land size	over 750m2	Unsure	unsure	760m2

(continued)

Table 8.1: your property checklist and research table (*cont'd*)

	Desired	Property 1	Property 2	Property 3
Layout	Don't care, maybe covered outdoor area	Open plan downstairs	The back patio is concrete without a cover. Can be added as others have an awning. Need to check.	No outdoor area, room though
Levels	Single preferred	2	2	Single
Living areas	Multiple	2	2, upstairs is large	2
Outdoor area	Flat backyard	Slight pitch	Reasonably flat	Flat
Deal breakers				
Build style	Brick	Brick	Brick downstairs, cladding upstairs	Brick
Title	Freehold (Torrens)	Strata, 8 in complex	Strata, 4 in complex	Freehold
Local school	<5km	Yes	Within catchment	None within 5km
Public transport	<5km	Yes	Yes	No
Infrastructure	Within 20 mins to M1	Yes	No	No
Café	Walkable less than 15 mins	Yes	Yes	No
Internet	Fibre to the node (FTTN)	Yes	No, but upgrade is due within 12 months. Currently FTTN	FTTN
Notes				
Strata sinking and admin fund		Some arrears	Healthy, no issues it seems.	n/a
Overall rating out of 10		6.5	8	7

	Desired	Property 1	Property 2	Property 3
Other		Bus stop right out the front. Looked like it would be annoying.	Made us think you can get something good, even if it's a townhouse. Lady to the left in no.7 was nice.	Has been renovated with the additional room and bathroom
Yes or No		No	Yes	No

You might see that as part of the research, property 1 had been and gone, but was vital to help form a view. On paper, the desired property leaned clearly towards a freestanding brick house with freehold title (property 3). That was the ideal. However, once a large number of properties was inspected in the target area, it became clear that holding too rigidly to a 'house only' rule was excluding otherwise strong options. Property 2, while a townhouse, met the majority of the hard considerations and evaded most of the deal-breakers. It was within budget, sat in the correct school catchment, was near new, had brick construction on the lower level and offered multiple living areas with a practical layout. The compromises were understood and manageable, rather than structural or financial red flags. Importantly, it was immediately liveable, not a property that required work straight after settlement.

This process helped separate genuine non-negotiables from preferences. After inspecting several townhouses that ticked the key boxes, it became clear that, in the right location and condition, a townhouse could be a sensible long-term option. By contrast, property 3 met some hard and soft considerations, including land size, location and layout, but ultimately failed on deal-breakers that couldn't be overlooked. The absence of nearby amenities, upcoming renovation requirements and weaker transport and lifestyle fit meant the trade-offs stacked up too heavily. In isolation, it wasn't a poor property. Against the agreed red lines, it was an easy no.

The research process may also give you a reality check that avoiding a deal-breaker or getting something you need isn't actually possible. That's also okay, as resetting expectations early can be a good thing.

> If Rach is looking at a house to live in, she looks straight at the kitchen because this is where she loves to spend time. But a beautiful kitchen could distract her from looking at all the features of the home. The truth is a kitchen can be remodelled. Some amazing appliances may distract her from noticing all the things she needs to take note of in the open home or inspection. Be aware of your own biases as you walk through properties!

Private treaty vs auction

Next we're going to outline the steps for buying via private treaty vs buying at auction. Figure 8.3 presents a comparison.

Buying via private treaty

Private treaty is the most common method of sale in Australia. It's also the most flexible because you get to negotiate not just price, but settlement period, inclusions and conditions. Every state handles this process differently, and your conveyancer can guide you on the correct steps for making offers.

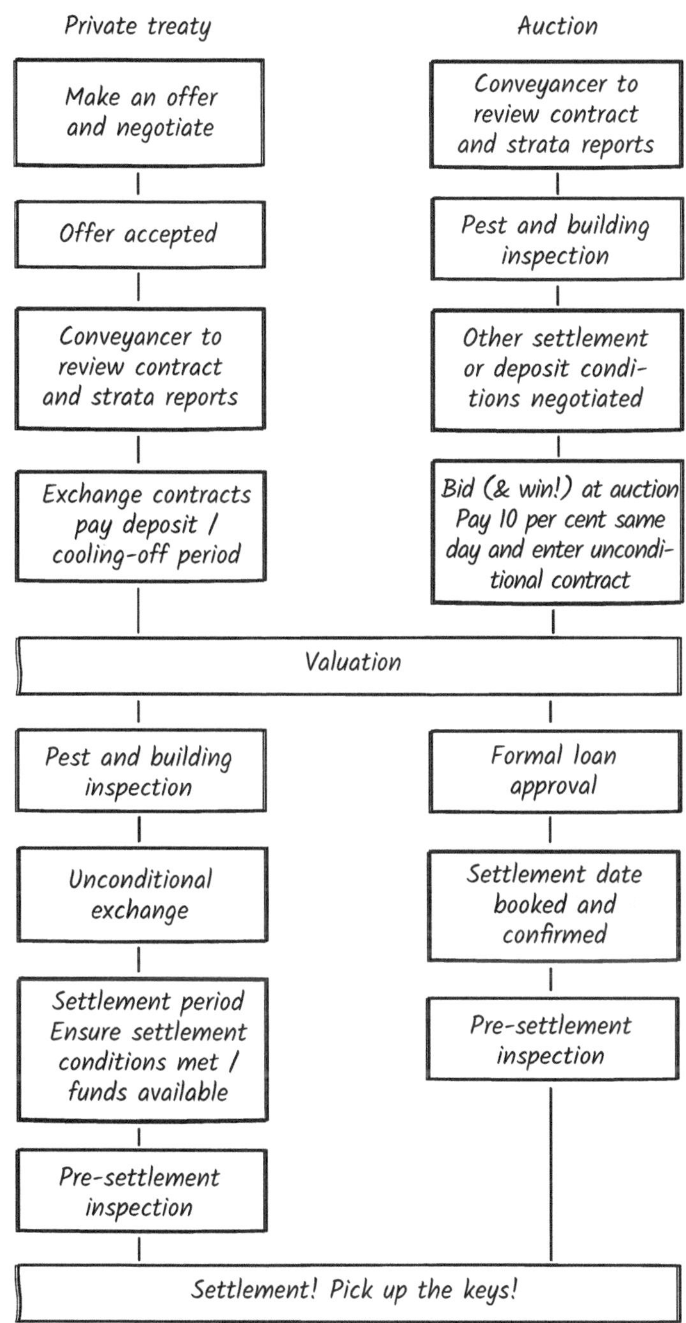

Figure 8.3: private treaty vs auction

Across Australia, private treaty sales allow negotiation on price, settlement length, inclusions and conditions. However, the treatment of offers is different across states:

- *NSW, Vic., SA, WA*: offers can be verbal or written. Agents must present all offers to the vendor
- *Qld*: offers are almost always made in the contract itself
- *NT and Tas.*: offers are typically written but informal until contract stage.

The conveyancer helps the buyer understand whether an offer is binding (Qld), subject to contract (NSW, Vic.) or subject to statutory conditions.

Here's how it plays out in real life.

MAKING AN OFFER AND NEGOTIATING

Once you've found a property you love, you contact the agent and make a formal offer, usually in writing. You include the price, your preferred settlement period and sometimes conditions such as finance or wanting a building and pest inspection. The agent will take your offer to the vendor. Sometimes they'll accept it. More often, they'll counteroffer. Negotiations can feel emotional, but remember: it's not personal. It's just a process of two parties trying to find the right number. At this stage, you should have spoken to your broker to ensure your offer sits safely within your pre-approval amount.

OFFER ACCEPTED

Once an offer is accepted, a common question is, 'What do I do now?' When the seller says yes, the pace suddenly accelerates. You move from thinking about it to 'I need to get everything lined up ASAP'.

But even when an offer is accepted, the property isn't yours yet. The contract hasn't been exchanged and until then, another buyer could potentially swoop in.

It's so important to understand that an offer being accepted doesn't secure you a property—*nothing* is final until the contracts have legally exchanged. Remember, this process is different for each state but you'll have had your conveyancer explain this, so that you're informed and know these rules before you get here.

There is often heartbreak and frustration when buyers feel wronged because someone else has offered a higher amount or, even worse, another buyer has swooped in and exchanged contracts without even giving you the option to increase your offer. Back to the rules of the game: the real estate agent works for the owner and their job is to get them the best price, but also to ensure the sale happens. Sometimes that means a cash buyer can completely shift the outcome because from the agent's perspective, they're a safer, faster option for the owner. Keep your team close and know the rules for your state. Have a game plan.

CONVEYANCER / SOLICITOR REVIEWS CONTRACT AND STRATA REPORT

Before you sign anything that's unconditional, your conveyancer goes through the contract with a fine-tooth comb. They check clauses, look for red flags, review strata reports, identify unusual conditions and ensure the terms are fair and standard. This step protects you from buying into hidden problems such as unresolved building works, major defects or weird easements.

When you're considering buying into a strata scheme, one of your first steps should be to obtain a comprehensive strata report and as much strata history as possible from the selling agent. Pay close attention to AGM notices/agendas and minutes as these reveal what the owners corporation is dealing with now and what may be coming next.

Two funds matter here. The administrative fund covers the day-to-day running costs such as insurance, cleaning, gardening, minor repairs, strata management fees and utilities. The capital works fund, formerly known as the sinking fund, is set aside for big-ticket items like roof replacements, lifts, concrete repairs, repainting and major structural works over the life of the building.

A major red flag is a capital works fund with little or no money, especially in older buildings, as this often means it isn't a matter of if but when a special levy will be needed.

Another warning sign is multiple lots being in arrears on their strata levies as this can strain cash flow and push costs onto owners who do pay on time. Also watch for upcoming strata meetings. If a meeting is due soon and past minutes show unresolved issues, it can be sensible to wait for the latest minutes before proceeding.

You'll need to kiss a lot of frogs and buy many strata reports before you buy your first property. Buyers usually pay for strata reports out of pocket (often costing them around $200 to $300), although some sellers provide them for free.

Your conveyancer or a specialist strata reviewer can help, but a smart first pass is to upload the full report into an AI tool and ask it to flag risks, future costs, levy pressure, disputes and anything that could materially affect affordability or resale.

Here's an example AI prompt you can use: 'Review this strata report and summarise any major risks, planned or upcoming works, special levy risks, building defects, disputes, legal issues, or unusually high or rising levies. Highlight anything that could materially impact costs or future resale'.

EXCHANGE OF CONTRACTS, PAYING THE DEPOSIT AND THE COOLING-OFF PERIOD

In a private treaty sale, exchange often happens in two steps. First, you sign the contract, pay a small deposit (sometimes as little as 0.25 per cent) and begin your cooling-off period. In most states, the cooling-off period is five *business* days (NSW), though Queensland has five days and other states vary. This window allows you to organise inspections and finance without losing the property to someone else.

If you walk away during cooling-off, you may lose a small percentage of the purchase price (usually 0.25 per cent in NSW), but it's significantly less than losing your entire deposit later.

If there is a cooling-off period the buyer is protected, as they can pull out, but the owner isn't protected: they can't accept a higher offer or change their mind.

In some states, such as Queensland, your exchange is subject to things like finance and pest and building inspection. Remember, you'll have a game plan with your conveyancer, who will be well versed in the rules that apply in your state.

VALUATION

Your lender sends a valuer to assess the property, but this may not always happen. A valuation isn't a full building inspection—it's checking whether the property is worth what you're paying. If the valuation comes in low, your broker will strategise how to cover the gap, renegotiate or approach other lenders. The valuation is there for the bank to check their security but also for you to check you aren't paying too much, so if there's an issue, talk to your team (coming up in chapter 9) about why.

PEST AND BUILDING INSPECTION

This is a non-negotiable. A qualified inspector checks structural integrity, pest activity, drainage issues, roof condition, electrical safety, plumbing and anything that could become expensive later. You don't want surprises, especially ones with termites.

In the ACT, these reports are automatically stipulated in the contract. In other states, there will be occasions when the owner gets the pest and building report done for you.

UNCONDITIONAL EXCHANGE AND PAYING THE REMAINING DEPOSIT

Once valuation, finance and inspections are sorted, you proceed to unconditional exchange. This is when you pay the balance of your deposit (usually 10 per cent of the purchase price) and the deal becomes legally binding. No turning back: this is the 'we're really doing it' moment.

SETTLEMENT PERIOD AND MEETING ALL CONDITIONS

The settlement period is usually 30 to 90 days. During this time:

- your lender organises the loan
- your conveyancer checks all legal requirements
- rates and adjustments are calculated
- your broker prepares for settlement day
- you coordinate any insurance required before settlement.

The property is still legally the seller's, but you're preparing to take ownership.

PRE-SETTLEMENT INSPECTION

This usually happens the day before, or the morning of, settlement. It's your chance to walk through the property and make sure everything included in the contract is still there; nothing has been damaged; all appliances, taps and lights are working; and any rubbish has been removed. Essentially, you're checking that the property is in the same condition as when you exchanged. If anything's not right, your conveyancer will step in to negotiate last-minute fixes.

> At the pre-settlement inspection, a key thing to understand is that the seller's obligation is limited. The property only needs to be in the same condition as when you inspected it and agreed to buy it. This inspection is not a last-minute chance to uncover new issues or renegotiate. If something important like the air conditioner, dishwasher or another included appliance wasn't working when you first viewed the property, that needed to be identified and addressed before contracts were exchanged. After exchange, the benchmark is simply 'as inspected', not 'perfect'.
>
> That said, if you arrive at the pre-settlement inspection and find something materially different or significantly worse, that's when you act. Think major damage, a hole in a wall, missing fixtures, rubbish left behind or signs of vandalism. In those situations, don't argue directly with the agent or the seller. Raise it immediately with your conveyancer or lawyer and follow their advice. This is exactly what they're there for and the goal is to protect your position before settlement goes through and the keys become your problem.

SETTLEMENT

On settlement day, your lender sends the funds, your conveyancer finalises the transfer and the property becomes legally yours. You get the keys, the title moves into your name and you're officially a homeowner. Take a photo. Celebrate. Cry happy tears. Call your mum. Be prepared for the unexpected here: things can happen that may delay settlement and it's not uncommon for these things to be out of your control. There are a lot of moving parts and your dream team (see chapter 9) will be there to help with the unexpected, if they come up.

Buying at auction

Buying at auction is exciting, intense and—let's be honest—a bit terrifying the first time. It's the fast, high-pressure, no-cooling-off version of buying a home. But it's also incredibly common in Australia, especially in competitive markets like Sydney and Melbourne. The big difference with the auction process is that when you buy at auction, you commit on the spot. No cooling-off, no finance clause, no 'let me check the contract'. Everything must be sorted *before* auction day.

> Rach has asked a friend to bid for her at auction in the past. It was an emotional purchase (buying her family home) and she didn't want to give away anything to the agent or the other bidders. Her friend knew her maximum bid and was also a real estate agent, so he had experience to lean on. If you use a buyer's agent, they can do this for you. Go to a few auctions before your own, so you see how they work. Watch how the real estate selling agents are running around and talking to the buyers encouraging them to bid and how the auctioneer controls events.

Here's how the process works.

1 CONTRACT AND STRATA REVIEW BEFORE THE AUCTION

Your conveyancer reviews the contract upfront because if you win, you sign it immediately. Any changes you might want need to be negotiated before auction day.

2 PEST AND BUILDING INSPECTION BEFORE AUCTION

Because auction purchases are unconditional, all due diligence must be done beforehand. That means paying for the inspection with no guarantee you'll buy the property. Frustrating sometimes, but essential.

3 OTHER SETTLEMENT OR DEPOSIT CONDITIONS

When buying at auction, any changes to the standard contract conditions must be negotiated well before auction day. This includes settlement terms, such as a shorter or longer settlement period, and deposit arrangements, like paying 5 per cent instead of 10 per cent on the day or using a deposit bond. These variations aren't informal side conversations. They must be formally agreed to and signed off by the seller, usually via the auctioneer, before the auction begins. If it isn't approved in writing beforehand, assume it won't be allowed.

The reason this matters is simple. Once you bid at auction and your offer is accepted, you're in an unconditional contract. There's no cooling-off period, no finance clause and no chance to renegotiate settlement or deposit terms after the hammer falls. At that point, everything is locked in. Do the negotiating early, get it documented and walk into auction day knowing exactly what you're committing to.

4 BID AT AUCTION

If you win, you sign the contract on the spot and pay the 10 per cent deposit (sometimes negotiated to 5 per cent, but only if agreed to in advance). There's no backing out. The contract is unconditional. You're locked in.

5 VALUATION

After the auction, your lender orders a valuation. Usually this is straightforward because the market essentially decides the value at auction, but occasionally valuations come in short. Your broker helps plan for this scenario before auction day so you're not blindsided. Some buyers with pre-approvals who are buying at high LVRs (let's say 95 per cent) may opt not to buy at auction due to the potential risk of a valuation being done after formal contracts. However, the risk is extremely low as generally the best way to determine a property's value is what it sells for under auction conditions.

6 FORMAL LOAN APPROVAL

Your lender finalises your loan documents and issues unconditional approval. With auctions, your broker will usually have you very close to unconditional approval beforehand to avoid stress.

7 SETTLEMENT DATE CONFIRMED

Settlement terms for auctions are set in advance (often up to 42 days). There's no negotiating after you win. Your broker and conveyancer coordinate all the legal and financial requirements to prepare for settlement. You continue saving as much as possible because a buffer helps reduce stress if costs come in slightly higher than anticipated.

8 PRE-SETTLEMENT INSPECTION

The same as you would when purchasing through private treaty, you inspect the property before settlement to ensure it's in acceptable condition.

9 SETTLEMENT

Funds transfer, ownership changes hands and you officially own the home. You pick up the keys, take the classic 'standing in front of the door' photo and let it all sink in.

> Auctions are one of the most intimidating parts of the property market for first-home buyers. They're fast, public, emotional and unforgiving. It's completely reasonable to feel overwhelmed by them. Auctions are designed to create urgency and competition, which can push buyers beyond their comfort zone if they're not prepared. For some first buyers, avoiding auctions altogether is a valid strategy, especially early on.
>
> If you do choose to participate, preparation is everything. A clear walk-away price, finance fully sorted and a plan for how you'll bid removes most of the risk. Winning an auction won't feel like a win if it causes financial stress later. Walking away isn't failure. In many cases, it's proof that you stayed in control. There will always be another property. There won't always be another chance to undo an overstretched decision.

Making offers and negotiating

Here's the golden rule of negotiation: if you tell the agent you'll go higher, chances are high that you will. Agents are legally obligated to achieve the highest price for the vendor, so it pays to keep your cards close and approach negotiations with a clear structure.

Before you start, make sure you know what the property is worth today; what the seller needs in terms of timing, conditions and price expectations; and how much interest there is from other potential buyers. Being prepared on these points gives you a much stronger negotiating position.

Questions to ask the real estate agent:

- Why is the owner selling?
- What's important to them: price, timing, conditions?
- How many contracts are out?
- Has the seller indicated a price range?

But there are also things you should *not* say to a real estate agent:

- We absolutely love it — whatever it takes!
- We're terrified of missing out.
- Our limit is $X. Is that enough?
- We'll definitely go higher if needed.

Keep it steady and keep it measured. Stay within your plan.

Submit your offer in writing

One of the best ways to demonstrate seriousness with a real estate agent is to submit your offer in writing. It demonstrates confidence. Nothing says 'I know what I'm doing' like a written offer. Some real estate agents will even accept this via text message.

Here's a simple template you can use:

Property address:	____________________
Buyers:	____________________
Offer price:	$___________________
Conditions: *(e.g. finance clause, deposit bond)*	____________________
Settlement period:	____________________
Conveyancer:	____________________

Agents *love* this because it's clear, complete and easy to present to the seller. It also takes away any possible chance of miscommunication.

Ultimately, when you strip away the noise, here's what matters:

- Agents work for the seller.
- You can still use the relationship strategically.
- You become the buyer they *want* to call.
- And you gain information and access others don't get.

When you stay prepared, confident, respectful and structured, you stop feeling overwhelmed and start feeling empowered. This is how first-home buyers take control — and how you become the buyer who actually gets the keys.

Property in action

Take some time to practise writing an offer for a potential property. Choose a property you might have looked at recently, or choose one now and practise writing an offer using the template.

How to know what a property is really worth

We often hear people ask, 'What's this property worth?' But how do you *actually* know? Especially when some properties don't list a price, or the range is as wide as the Grand Canyon! The good news is, with a bit of research, you can get a realistic idea and it will give you confidence when negotiating.

A few tips to help you get real numbers:

- *Ask your mortgage broker*: Your broker has access to valuation tools that show comparable sales in the area. Even without a full valuation, they can give you a price range. If you're unsure about a property, ask your broker to run a report.

- *Use real estate apps wisely*: Everyone scrolls listings, but the 'sold' section is gold. Search for similar properties in the area and sort by 'most recent'. If the price isn't listed, call the agent — don't be shy! They'll tell you what it sold for and you might even get a heads-up on similar properties coming to market.

- *Spend time in the local market*: The more homes you see and track through to sale, the better you'll understand local values. We know property hunting can be exhausting, but even casually watching the market helps you build knowledge, spot trends and form relationships with agents — all before you need to make your first offer.

- *Consider a buyer's agent*: Not everyone has the time to research the market properly. A buyer's agent can save you hours and in tricky markets, they're worth every cent. For first-home buyers, your deposit might limit this option, but it's good to know it exists as a tool for the future.

Knowing a property's real value isn't just about numbers, it's about confidence. The more you research, the stronger your negotiating position will be.

It's a lot, but you've got this

The buying process in Australia has many moving parts and it's normal to feel overwhelmed at times. But with the right information, a supportive team and a clear plan, the journey becomes far more manageable.

There are a million scenarios and tips we would love to share, but it's impossible to cover everything that will come up. What we really want you to understand at this stage is that getting the right advice is important. Whether it's a buyer's agent, mortgage broker or conveyancer, these people are important members of your team and you need to have the right ones and be able to ask the important questions to avoid any potential issues.

Every successful first-home buyer starts exactly where you are now: with questions, uncertainties and the desire to make informed decisions. As you take each step, the path becomes clearer. And by the time you reach settlement, you'll understand the process deeply enough to know you earned every part of the achievement.

Buying your first home isn't just a financial decision. It's a milestone that shapes your future. And now you have the roadmap to navigate it with confidence.

Start with this...

The buying process is one of the newest parts of this journey for you! Start to get familiar by:

- determining what part of the property cycle one of your preferred suburbs is currently in
- practising writing an offer for a property, or going to watch an auction that's local to you. The more you see and practice, the better.

Why you need a dream team

Your team is your biggest asset. A smart mortgage broker, a solid conveyancer, maybe a buyer's agent if that fits your plan. They will form your personal dream team! These people can be the difference between a smooth ride and a costly mess. Earlier chapters explained deposits, borrowing power and timelines. Now the real action starts. Your crew is in place, your strategy is set and your finger is hovering over the 'book inspection' button.

Some first-home buyers think, 'How hard can it be? I'll just research online and figure it out'. And look, you *can* do that. In the same way you can cut your own hair, assemble flat-pack furniture without instructions or diagnose yourself via Google Doctor. But doing something yourself doesn't mean doing it well, or safely.

Buying your first home is a major financial decision with long-term consequences. You need clarity and you need protection. And you need people who spend their entire careers understanding things you don't have the time (or desire) to master.

Your dream team brings:

- *expertise* you can lean on
- *experience* you don't have
- *communication* that calms and guides you
- *protection* from mistakes that cost tens of thousands
- *perspective* when emotions run high.

And maybe most importantly, a good team saves you from feeling completely overwhelmed.

Because no matter how independent or capable you are, this process is not intuitive. It's not 'common sense'. You're not meant to magically know how lenders think, how to read contracts, how to negotiate with agents or how to spot hidden structural issues. Your team does. And they care about protecting you because your first home should feel like a milestone, not a minefield.

Meet your dream team: The people who carry you through the journey

Let's break down who you actually need around you. Not everyone needs the full suite, but these are the core professionals who create a smooth, safe, confident buying process.

Finding your dream team works the same way as you find a good hairdresser or a mechanic you actually trust. You ask people who have already been there and had a good experience. Word of mouth is gold. Google reviews and online referrals can help, but they're a starting point, not a decision maker.

The bigger point is this: When you're choosing professionals like mortgage brokers, accountants, financial advisers, lawyers or buyer's agents, you want people who work with people just like you. If you owned an old European car, you wouldn't take it to the local Toyota dealer. Buying your first property is no different. Experience matters, but relevant experience matters more.

Follow the QR code on page 300, which has links to resources from trusted people and businesses we know Australia wide, saving you time and mistakes. Use those as a shortcut, then still do your own sense check. The right team should understand your situation, your budget and your stage of life, not treat you like just another transaction.

Mortgage broker

Your mortgage broker is usually your first call and your longest lasting relationship in the buying process. If there's no buyer's agent in the mix, the mortgage broker is the 'project manager' of the purchase leading the other members of the team and reaching out to keep everyone in touch.

> It's worth noting that mortgage brokers are bound by best interest duty (BID) and must act in your best interest. In rare cases, you might need to go to the bank directly and if this is the case the mortgage broker will tell you. For example, the Shared Equity scheme trial in Victoria in 2025 wasn't offered to mortgage brokers and there were cases that had to be referred to the bank directly.

Conveyancer / solicitor

If the broker is the finance expert, the conveyancer (or property solicitor) is the legal expert. They review the contract of sale, check the title, explain clauses, look for hidden risks and make sure the property you're buying is legally sound. Unlike your mortgage broker, who can be located anywhere, your conveyancer needs to be in the state where you're buying. Every state is different and has different rules and things to look out for.

Our top tip is to meet with your conveyancer before you start looking at properties. Get a game plan together and understand everything you need to look out for. You're going to make offers and need to sign contracts and your conveyancer will be the person who explains the conditions around signing.

After you've exchanged contracts, the conveyancer has a lot more work to do. Property contracts are long, technical and full of conditions that can make or break your experience. Your conveyancer:

- reviews the contract
- checks the title
- identifies risks
- manages deadlines
- handles the legal steps of settlement
- communicates with the seller's legal team.

They are your protector. Their job is to make sure you don't sign anything dangerous, unfair or financially disastrous.

SHOULD I USE A CONVEYANCER OR A SOLICITOR?

It really comes down to personal preference and your situation. A conveyancer specialises solely in property transactions, reviewing contracts, checking titles and managing settlement, and is often more affordable. A solicitor can do all of that too, but may charge more and can be useful if your purchase is more complex (think unusual contract conditions, trusts or legal disputes). For most first-home buyers buying a standard property, a conveyancer is usually sufficient, but if in doubt, it's worth getting advice early so you feel confident and protected. A conveyancer will let you know if your transaction requires a solicitor. They may even recommend one.

If you're looking at multiple properties, some conveyancers may allow reviews of a few contracts within the fee, so you don't have to cough up another cost each time. Generally, this amount is lodged as a cost on settlement, so you don't need to pay the money from your bank account.

Buyer's agent (optional, but powerful)

Buyer's agents (sometimes called buyers advocates) work solely for you — not the seller — and can be an incredibly powerful ally in the buying process. They help you find suitable properties, research suburbs, evaluate the market, negotiate on price and even represent you at auctions. One of their underrated benefits is protecting you from emotional, rushed or biased decision making, which can easily creep in when you're buying a home. They're especially valuable if you're time poor, feeling overwhelmed by the process or simply want someone in your corner who does this every single day.

Not everyone will use a buyer's agent as they are an optional additional cost, but they can add a lot of value and are becoming more common each year. In writing this book, we presume that the average reader will *not* have a buyer's agent, but if you'd like to outsource the property search and negotiation to a professional, you'll want to hire one.

For many first-home buyers already struggling to get the deposit amount needed a buyer's agent is likely to be too expensive. If you're a personality type that struggles to stay calm in high-pressure situations, consider partnering with a buyer's agent from the beginning, if you can. A good buyer's agent will partner with you, forward plan with you and execute the best strategy to secure the right home for you at the best price and terms possible. Costs for their services vary, but a percentage of the purchase price is a good place to start (expect generally around the 2 per cent mark). On an $800 000 property purchase that's $16 000. When you're already scraping together a deposit and other costs, this can't always be achieved.

> A quick note: there are buyer's agents out there who work exclusively with property investors, so if buying an investment property first is your goal, look for an agent who has experience specifically with investors.

WHAT BUYER'S AGENTS DO

A great buyer's agent:

- *should offer more than just property searching.* They should sit with you to learn more about your life, forward plan with you, understand how life may evolve over three-to-five and 10+ years, learn how you live inside and outside of the home and then begin matching you with the right homes in the right locations. A detailed brief will be created to match your budget, along with your requirements, and then they will enter the marketplace to begin sourcing. When negotiating begins they should also be going in to bat for you.

- *should have excellent local expertise and market knowledge.* They should be able to guide you to the most desirable streets, school catchments and most importantly the areas to avoid. A good buyer's agent will also have a comprehensive understanding of recent sales, agent activity, demographics and future developments in the area they service. A good buyer's agent will have a proven track record and results: look at how many properties they've purchased in the past 6 to 12 months, especially in your budget range and desired location. Check client reviews and testimonials.

- *should have strong relationships with other key stakeholders and have strong professional networks*. Their networks are often how you get access to pre-market and off-market opportunities and also help you act with speed and confidence when the right opportunity is presented.

- *should be responsive, approachable, available and easy to communicate with*. If, after speaking with them, you feel they've listened closely, asked the right questions and already given you insight into the market, you're likely in good hands.

We went into a lot of detail here because buyer's agents, like mortgage brokers, can have very low entry requirements and we see ever more people giving advice who shouldn't. As with your other professionals, check you're working with someone experienced and with proven results, not just someone who has a great TikTok account.

> Rach once worked with clients Steph and James, who had been searching for three months in a hot market where supply was low. After repeatedly missing out, they hired a local buyer's agent. Within one week, the agent secured them an off-market property through industry connections. They were relieved, supported and able to refocus on their jobs, which had suffered during their intense search.

For the investors

If your first property is likely to be an investment, there are a few other professionals you will want to consider having on your team.

Accountant

It's worth speaking with an accountant before you sign anything. They can help you think through the best ownership structure, explain how depreciation schedules work and walk you through the implications of negative gearing and capital gains tax. They'll also help you understand the expected after-tax cost of holding the property so you're not surprised down the track. Most first-time investors end up buying in their personal names, but it's still worth understanding the alternatives before you commit.

Property manager

When an investor has identified an area of interest, one of the next steps should be selecting the best property manager operating locally. Their insight into the rental market is grounded in everyday experience: leasing properties, speaking with tenants, dealing with maintenance issues, and monitoring supply and demand trends. This makes them an invaluable source of intelligence long before a contract is signed.

A good property manager can outline which property types are renting well, what local tenants consistently prioritise and whether certain streets or pockets of the suburb tend to perform better than others. When an investor is considering a specific property, the property manager can offer an informed opinion about its rental appeal, potential risks or practical considerations that may not be obvious during an inspection. They can also flag issues common to the neighbourhood, such as parking shortages, noise complaints, ageing infrastructure or planned developments that may influence future demand.

For investors building a property rather than purchasing an established one, involving a property manager early can streamline the entire handover process. They can coordinate directly with the builder to arrange pre-settlement inspections, ensure all keys and access devices are accounted for, collect warranty documentation and prepare the property for its first tenants. This early involvement reduces delays and helps achieve a faster transition from completion to rental income.

Some investors choose to self-manage to save costs, but this decision should be weighed carefully. A common pattern among investors who report stressful or unsuccessful rental experiences is that they managed the property themselves. Professional property managers provide structure, compliance oversight and a buffer between the investor and the tenant, which is particularly useful when repairs, arrears or disputes arise.

A property manager's responsibilities extend well beyond finding tenants. They handle advertising, screen applications, conduct reference checks, prepare leases, collect rent, manage inspections, arrange maintenance, ensure legal compliance, handle vacate processes and represent the owner when issues escalate. A good manager protects both the property and the investor's time while supporting a positive experience for tenants.

In short, selecting the right property manager early helps investors make informed decisions, reduces risk and lays the foundation for a smoother, more professional investment experience.

Be thorough when choosing one. Look for:

- strong systems
- manageable workload
- good communication
- positive reviews.

Overloaded property managers often miss important details, something Glen has lived experience with (keep reading ...).

Glen recently had a breakup (not in the romantic sense), with one of his property managers. The rent roll was sold (that's industry term for all the business's customers), the new agency took over and the whole thing slid into a slow-moving train wreck of sloppy systems, poor communication and basic details getting missed. We're talking about multiple new managers ringing him about properties they already manage, rent renewals that weren't due, rent increases that apparently happened (but also ... didn't), trades leaving holes in ceilings and emails bouncing because they changed their domain without telling anyone. Death by a thousand cuts.

The caution for anyone with investment properties is simple: pay attention to your manager's systems, workload and communication. If they're dropping the ball with you, they're probably dropping it with your tenants and that reflects on you. Ask how many properties they each manage, look for consistency and don't be afraid to reset when the grace period drags beyond reasonable. Your tenants deserve better and so do you.

Property coach

For an investor, an alternative to a buyers' agent — or at times used with a buyers' agent — can be a property coach. Property coaches help you establish your 'why' and your investment strategy. They may educate you on how to find a property rather than find the property for you like a buyers' agent would. Your choice will likely depend on your budget (not everyone can afford a buyers' agent) and your desire to learn, the time you have available, your interest and your confidence to do the research yourself (some people love to get the education and then buy themselves).

Note: beware of the property coach who is paid by the developer. How can they have your strategy at the forefront of their goals when they only get paid if they sell a particular developer's stock?

Your support squad (friends, family, mentors)

They don't need qualifications; they just need perspective. Buying your first home can stir up doubt, fear, comparison and overwhelm. Having people who can remind you of your goals and help you stay grounded matters massively.

Additional supporting roles

Some buyers will also need:

- *a strata report provider*: for apartments/townhouses
- *an insurance provider*: for home and contents insurance
- *a valuer*: arranged by the bank
- *a financial adviser*: for long-term planning.

Property in action

Find a mortgage broker you can have an initial discussion with. They might be local to you, referred by a friend or you might reach out to Rach's team at Sphere Home Loans.

How to understand and work with real estate agents

We asked a lot of first-home buyers what they wished they knew before they started their buying journey, and a very common theme was negative experiences with real estate agents or not knowing the rules of play before they started.

The part of the buying process that drains first-home buyers more than anything else is dealing with real estate agents. The calls, the questions, the pressure, the 'Are you ready to make an offer today?' — it's a lot. But once you understand how agents work and what motivates them, the whole experience becomes a *lot* easier. And, dare we say, empowering.

THE ONE THING EVERY BUYER NEEDS TO KNOW

The real estate agent works for the seller, not you. Legally, contractually, financially, morally (well ... sort of). Their job is to get the owner the best possible price and the best possible outcome. So, when they use tactics to nudge you up in price or push you to act quickly, that's not them being dodgy, that's them doing their job. Once you understand this, you stop taking things personally and start playing the game strategically.

Even though real estate agents represent the vendor, they can still be a huge advantage to you, if you know how to work with them. The goal isn't to 'beat' them; it's to build a respectful, professional relationship where they recognise you as a serious buyer. When that happens, they're far more likely to keep you in mind and share information or opportunities earlier than they would with the average person. Think of it as positioning yourself as the buyer an agent *wants* to talk to.

HOW TO SHOW AGENTS YOU'RE A SERIOUS BUYER

Agents are human. They want to help. But they don't want to waste time on buyers who aren't ready. If you want to be on their 'serious buyer' list, you need to demonstrate that you're ready to buy. Here's how:

- *Be fully pre-approved and make sure they know it.* Tell them your broker and conveyancer are standing by.

- *Share your price range (a range, not your limit).* They don't need your ceiling.

- *Chat at open homes.* Not in a forced fake-networking way, just introduce yourself and tell them what you're looking for.

- *Share your non-negotiables.* Agents can't match you with properties if they don't know your brief.

This sets you apart immediately from the vast majority of 'just-looking' buyers. A good agent will quickly pick up on things like how urgently you want to buy, how emotional you are, how confident you seem and whether you know your budget and limits. This isn't good or bad; it's simply part of how they read the room. Your job is to stay calm, confident and clear.

WHY AGENTS ASK SO MANY QUESTIONS AT OPEN HOMES

We know the follow-up calls after open homes can be exhausting. But agents ask all those questions because they're required to give the vendor weekly feedback. That feedback covers things like how many people came through the property, what buyers think it's worth, what other homes they're comparing it to and any objections that came up during inspections.

Agents may ask:

- Are your finances ready?
- Are you prepared to sign if accepted?
- What settlement conditions do you need?
- Will you need a deposit bond?

This isn't them being nosy—it's them protecting the sale. A collapsed sale is a nightmare for an agent and the owner. The last thing they want to do is lose another buyer to a buyer who wasn't actually ready. So, when you tell an agent 'Nah, not for me', and they still push for more details, they're not trying to trap you, they're just doing their job. Give them thoughtful, specific feedback and they'll remember you. It shows you're realistic, switched on and you understand the market. They might also have other properties on their list that match what you're after.

LEVERAGING AGENT RELATIONSHIPS AND AIMING FOR A WIN-WIN

After a few weekends of open homes, you'll naturally start seeing the same faces. Use this to your advantage. You don't have to get to know every agent in every office—just focus on one agent per office with whom you 'click'. Ideally, this will be someone who communicates well, isn't overly busy or dismissive, seems motivated in a positive way and actually listens.

Often, the 'up-and-comer' agents are the best choice, as they usually have the time and drive to help. Let them know you're hoping to buy through their office and want to be kept updated: it benefits both you and them because agents work on commission. In many offices, one agent lists the home while a different agent may handle the sale and they split the commission—unless the same agent does both.

So, if you're working closely with an agent, they may earn a cut just for introducing you to the property. That's why some agents go out of their way to keep you updated: they're investing in a potential sale. This is also how buyers often get early access, off-market opportunities and first looks.

WHAT YOU CAN ACCESS THROUGH AGENT RELATIONSHIPS

Once you're on agents' radars as a serious, easy-to-work-with buyer, new opportunities start to open up. You'll hear about homes before they're advertised, get calls about off-market properties and receive honest feedback about pricing and competition. You may also learn details about a seller's situation, like whether they want a quick sale or a flexible settlement, which can give you a stronger negotiating position. This doesn't mean the agent is on your team, but having that access gives you more information and more power.

Building and pest inspectors

A building and pest inspector is the person who goes where you would rather not. Into the roof cavity, under the floors, around the plumbing and through every corner of the property. Their job is to make sure you're not unknowingly buying a lemon. They look for signs of termites, water damage, unstable foundations, leaks and any unapproved or poorly done renovations that could come back to hurt you later. They will also flag likely future repair costs so you walk into the purchase with your eyes open, not crossed fingers.

In many cases, a good inspector can save buyers tens of thousands of dollars by identifying issues before contracts are locked in. You would typically expect to pay around $1000 for a comprehensive building and pest inspection. The report will come with plenty of disclaimers and limited liability, which is standard. The point is not that the property is perfect. (You might already know it's old and needs work.) The value of the inspector is catching the things you can't see, or wouldn't recognise as a serious problem, like what genuinely bad foundations actually look like. They're not exactly part of your dream team, but they offer a plug-in service that helps with your due diligence.

Table 9.1 depicts a summary of each professional you need on your team, their role, how to find one and the approximate cost.

Table 9.1: overall summary of your dream-team members

Professional	What they do	When you need them	How to find a good one	Approx. cost
Mortgage broker	Assesses borrowing power, runs scenarios, compares lenders, structures your loan, submits applications, manages the process from start to settlement and beyond. Often acts as the 'project manager' if no buyer's agent is involved	At the beginning—ideally before looking at properties	Personal referrals, podcasts (like 'this is property'), online reviews or recommendations from conveyancers / accountants. Look for someone who explains, not just sells	Usually *$0 upfront*. They are paid commission by the lender after settlement

(continued)

Table 9.1: overall summary of your dream-team members (*cont'd*)

Professional	What they do	When you need them	How to find a good one	Approx. cost
Conveyancer / property solicitor	Reviews contracts, checks the title, explains clauses, manages legal risk, handles settlement, liaises with seller's legal team	Before making offers on a property	Must be based in the *state you're buying in*. Ask brokers or buyers' agents for referrals. Look for responsiveness and clear communication	~$1200–$2500 depending on state and complexity
Buyers' agent (optional)	Searches for properties, assesses value, negotiates, bids at auction, provides market insight, removes emotion from decisions. Works only for the buyer	Optional—useful if time-poor, overwhelmed or buying in a competitive market	Look for proven results, local expertise, clear fee structure, strong referrals. Avoid agents selling stock	*~2 per cent of purchase price* (e.g. ~$16 000 on $800k property) or fixed fee

Professional	What they do	When you need them	How to find a good one	Approx. cost
Accountant (investors)	Advises on ownership structure, tax implications, negative gearing, depreciation, long-term tax planning	Before buying an investment property and ongoing each financial year	Referral from broker or other investors. Look for property experience, not just general tax	~$300–$600 for initial advice, plus annual tax fees
Property manager (investors)	Manages tenants, rent, maintenance, inspections, compliance and day-to-day operations	Early—ideally before buying and definitely before settlement	Local agencies with manageable portfolios, strong systems and good communication. Ask how many properties each manager handles	~6–9 per cent of weekly rent + letting fees
Property coach (optional, investors)	Helps clarify your 'why', investment strategy and education. May guide rather than source property directly	Early strategy phase, often before engaging a buyers' agent	Fee-for-service coaches. Avoid those paid by developers or selling specific stock	~$2000–$10 000+ depending on service level

Start with this…

Now is the time to start building your dream team!

* Do you have any potential referrals from friends or family for a mortgage broker or conveyancer? Give them a call and see if you can have an initial conversation.
* Would a buyer's advocate be within your budget? If not, think through how you will reach out to real estate agents yourself to broaden your property search.
* Ensure you've set up the appropriate budget for each professional you need.

10

You now have the keys — what's next?

Buying your first property is a huge milestone, but it's really just the beginning of your journey as a property owner. Once the contract is signed and the keys are in your hand, a whole new set of decisions and responsibilities comes into play. From understanding ongoing costs and managing maintenance, to planning renovations, using equity to invest further or eventually releasing parental guarantees — these are the next steps that can shape your financial future.

In this chapter, we'll walk you through what to expect after settlement, practical ways to protect your investment and strategies to make your property work for you over time. Think of it as the playbook for life after your first home.

Owning your first property is exciting, but it's easy to let your mortgage feel like it's in control. The good news? With some planning, you can manage your mortgage like a pro and reduce the years it takes to pay it off.

Manage your mortgage like a pro

Start by making your mortgage work for you, not the other way around. Ask yourself:

- Do you have an offset account?
- Do you have more than one offset account?
- Are your salary and savings working every day to reduce your interest?

Consider whether your loan is split or fixed and take note of any expiry dates. Your mortgage broker can help explain all these options. If you don't fully understand how your loans and accounts work at this stage, book a follow-up meeting. Have your internet banking ready and make sure you leave feeling confident about your repayments, offset accounts and how everything functions.

Sometimes first-home buyers get caught up in searches, approvals and negotiations and don't focus on managing their mortgage. Don't stress, your broker is there for you after settlement to make sure you're in control.

Tips to pay down your loan faster:

- Set higher repayments if you can.
- Make lump-sum contributions whenever possible.
- Use your offset accounts strategically to reduce interest and shorten your loan term.

Even small changes can shave years off your mortgage and save tens of thousands in interest.

Managing your money post-purchase

Once you finally get the keys, it can feel like the pressure cooker has been switched off. Months or years of saving, sacrifice and hyper-focus suddenly end and that's when spending can quietly run off the rails. Whether you're moving into the property or not, resist the urge to do everything at once. If it's your home, live in it for a while before making big decisions. Let the seasons change, see how the space actually functions and work out what you truly need rather than what feels urgent on day one. If it's an investment property, the same principle applies. Do nothing drastic. Let the dust settle, get the tenant in, make sure the rent, repayments and expenses are all flowing as expected and allow the property to find its rhythm before you start changing things.

The bigger risk after settlement is not the property itself—it's what happens to your money habits. Once the goal is achieved, the pressure valve releases and discipline can slip. That's when good systems slowly unravel. Whether you live in the home or hold it as an investment, this is the moment to lock in a new normal. Keep an emergency fund. Update your spending plan to include rates, insurance, maintenance and any holding costs, even if the numbers are educated guesses at first. Managing your money post-purchase shouldn't look wildly different from pre-purchase. The structure stays—only the line items change. Get this right and the property supports your life and strategy, rather than becoming a source of stress.

> Borrowing money to furnish or renovate is a common trap for first-time homeowners. After moving in, it's tempting to buy furniture and make your home perfect, but borrowing for these things can create huge stress. Credit cards, personal loans or 'interest-free' plans may seem harmless, but they can double the cost of items such as a $4000 lounge. Many first-home buyers end up refinancing or using home equity to pay off this debt, rather than accelerating mortgage repayments or investing in ways that grow wealth. Focus on maintaining your property and your financial stability in the first year.

Ongoing costs

You've focused heavily on saving a deposit and getting loan approval and now you have your keys (or investment property), but a new set of expenses also begins. Ideally, you've budgeted for these costs before buying, but it's important to understand and plan for them as you move forward.

MORTGAGE REPAYMENTS

This is generally your biggest ongoing cost. Early in your mortgage, so much of your monthly repayment is interest that it can feel particularly challenging.

A few tips to manage your mortgage effectively:

- *Plan an annual review with your mortgage broker*: check in regularly. If you haven't reviewed your loan in the past year, book a session.

- *Avoid unnecessary refinance traps*: refinancing every few years without checking the term can reset your loan to 30 years each time, costing more interest over time. If you refinance, consider reducing the term (for example, refinance at three years and reset to 27 years, or less).

- *Repayment strategy*: you can set repayments higher or make lump-sum contributions to reduce the term without locking yourself in.
- *Redraw accounts*: do you save in it or use it? Consider turning off access if the funds are tempting.
- *Offset accounts*: treat your offset as a high-interest, tax-free savings account. Money here reduces your home-loan balance and saves interest, unlike a taxed savings account.

See table 10.1 for a summary of the ongoing costs of owning a property.

Table 10.1: ongoing costs: what to expect

Cost component	Payment frequency	Estimated cost	Details
Home and contents insurance	Annually or monthly	National average $2795 for a combined policy; however, North Queensland, for example, is $4624	Mandatory for settlement. Protects the building structure and contents. Costs vary based on location, property age, value and level of coverage. Check the premium using the address of the proposed property prior to committing as it may impact your decision. Premiums can vary greatly between streets and different zoning, such as flood zones

(continued)

Table 10.1: ongoing costs: what to expect (*cont'd*)

Cost component	Payment frequency	Estimated cost	Details
Council rates	Quarterly	Variable based on property and should be available from selling agent or you can check with council	A local government property tax based primarily on the unimproved land value to fund local services
Water rates	Quarterly	Variable based on usage and fixed charges	Includes charges for water consumption and potentially a fixed service charge
Strata / body corporate fees	Quarterly	Variable (if applicable to units / townhouses)	Covers the maintenance, insurance and upkeep of common areas in strata-titled properties
Maintenance and repairs	As needed	Budget ~1 per cent of the property value annually (e.g. a $6000 budget for a $600 000 property)	Essential for covering routine upkeep and unexpected repairs
Utilities	Monthly / quarterly	Variable based on usage	Covers ongoing costs for electricity, gas and internet
Land tax (investors)	Annually	Variable	Tax applies in most states; calculated on the unimproved value of the land and increases as property values rise

Property in action

Take this opportunity to reshape your spending plan or budget. Ensure you've factored in new property ownership costs and consider what comes next in your property strategy. Start lining yourself up now!

Wills, estate planning and life insurance

In chapter 2, we talked about foundations, including wills, powers of attorney and personal insurances. If those boxes still aren't ticked, owning a property is your nudge to act, not a reason to panic. Buying a home or investment property usually means taking on debt and often it means other people rely on your income. That's when the risk is real. This is the point where life insurance and income protection stop being theoretical and start being practical. If something happens to you, the bank doesn't pause the mortgage out of sympathy.

If you have debt or dependants, life insurance matters. It's about making sure the people you care about aren't forced into selling under pressure or scrambling to cover repayments. Income protection is just as important. Your ability to earn an income is the engine that keeps everything running. Losing that income, even temporarily, can unravel your plans very quickly. These are not products to guess your way through. Getting the structure and the cover right depends on your situation, your cash flow and how your property fits into the bigger picture.

This is where speaking with a financial adviser is critical. They can help you work out what cover you actually need, what you don't and how it all fits together without crushing your budget. Follow the

QR code on page 300, for recommendations to help you get started if you don't have these insurances in place. Think of this as locking the doors after you've moved in. It's not exciting, but it protects everything you've worked so hard to build.

The power of valuations

You now own an asset that goes up (hopefully) in value. As this asset goes up in value you can use that to your advantage. Keeping up to date with what your property is worth can be of value to you in several ways:

- *Releasing a parental guarantee.* If you used a parental guarantee to get into the market have it released as soon as you can! This can be done when the value has increased and the loan has decreased and depending on your profession you can release it at 80 or 90 per cent with no LMI.

- *Releasing the government guarantee scheme.* If you used the First Home Guarantee scheme or similar the government is attached to your loan until you release them. Like the parental guarantee, this can be released when your loan is equal to 80 per cent or 90 per cent, depending on your occupation. Releasing the guarantee will take away the restrictions on your property such as not being able to rent it out.

- *Lowering your interest rate.* The lower your risk to the bank, the lower you may be able to negotiate your rate. If you borrow at 95 per cent LVR and your valuation means you now only owe 80 per cent of the value, you may be able to ask for a lower rate. Your mortgage broker should assess this at your annual reviews, but you need to know this as well to ensure that everyone is working on your behalf.

Releasing guarantees

Your mortgage broker may pro-actively contact you or it may come up in your annual review, but don't wait. If you think your property has increased in value enough to release your family member, reach out and organise a valuation. Your broker will organise this with no cost to you.

Depending on the bank or lender, you may need to show income and affordability at the time you're releasing the guarantee so if you're planning on taking time off for parental leave or becoming self-employed you may wish to address this guarantee prior to this, or at least discuss with the guarantor their expected time frames and wishes.

Renovations

There are three main reasons you may choose to renovate:

1. *To add value.* Increasing the valuation of your property gives you instant equity and allows you to utilise the equity you've built. You may use this to release a family or government guarantee, buy an investment property, or simply for peace of mind that your loan is now lower in comparison to the value of your property.

2. *To make it your own.* Renovations allow you to create the space you want to live in and tailor the property to your lifestyle and preferences.

3. *To get into a better area.* Fixing up a lower grade property in an area you're happy with for now may give you the boost you need to move to the next property you want to live in longer term.

Knowing your 'why' when you choose to renovate will help guide how you go about it and what you choose to improve.

Understanding the costs

Before starting any renovation, it's crucial to understand the full costs involved. Factor in materials, approvals, labour, project management, time, bad weather and unexpected issues that may arise. Knowing the total cost upfront helps you avoid surprises and ensures your renovation adds value rather than becoming a financial burden. This is where planning is key!

Financing a renovation

Many property owners use the equity in their home to fund renovations. This allows you to access funds without needing to save the entire amount upfront. Consider the end value of the property after renovations: will the improvements give you enough equity or value increase to justify the cost? Add value in a way that actually adds value.

How handy are you?

If you're handy and undertaking some work yourself, this can reduce costs. However, ensure you're realistic about your skills and the time required. There's nothing worse than burning out trying to save cash — sometimes it's best just to pay a professional! Poor DIY work can also reduce the value added or create costly fixes later, so ensure your skills are up to the task.

When do I need council approval?

Some renovations require council approval, especially structural changes, extensions or alterations to the property's exterior. Approval rules vary greatly by location, so it's essential to check with your local council before starting any work. Even minor renovations can trigger requirements depending on zoning, heritage overlays or building codes. Always confirm early to avoid fines, delays or costly modifications.

Planning and project management

Good planning is key. Create a timeline, set a budget and consider hiring a project manager if the renovation is complex. Keep track of contractors, deliveries and permits to avoid delays and unexpected costs.

The emotional side of renovations

Renovating a home can be exciting, but it's also stressful. Even small projects can uncover unexpected issues: unplanned wet weather days, structural surprises or trades that cost you more than you expected. It's easy to get frustrated, anxious or overwhelmed when things don't go perfectly according to plan.

Practical tips to ease the emotional challenge:

- *Set realistic expectations:* prepare yourself mentally for delays, extra costs or minor hiccups. These are annoying, but normal. Anticipating bumps in the road helps reduce stress when they happen.

- *Plan and budget carefully:* realistic budgets with buffers and timelines make surprises easier to handle. These also help you conceptualise what's coming next. Include a contingency fund for unexpected expenses.

- *Break the process into stages:* determine what steps come in what order. You don't have to do everything at once and naturally there'll be steps that have to come before others.

- *Communicate clearly with your builder or contractor:* pick a builder you communicate well with and encourage regular updates to help avoid misunderstandings and keep the project on track.

- *Keep your 'why' front of mind:* remember why you're renovating, whether it's for value, lifestyle or future flexibility. Focusing on the end goal helps you ride out temporary frustrations.

- *Take breaks and step back:* step back and go and do something fun every once in a while! Renovations can become all-consuming and it's easy to lose perspective.

Renovations test both patience and creativity, but with planning, clear communication and emotional awareness, the process can be much smoother and more enjoyable. Here are our top 5 value-add renovation ideas:

1. **Kitchens:** Upgrading benchtops, cabinets, appliances and lighting gives the biggest bang for your buck and modernises the heart of the home.

2. **Bathrooms:** Even small improvements like new taps, showers, vanities or tiles can significantly increase appeal and value.

3. **Fresh paint:** Neutral colours throughout the home brighten the space and make it feel well maintained.

4. **Flooring:** New carpets in bedrooms or modern timber/ laminate floors in living areas lift the overall look and feel.

5. **Curb appeal and outdoor spaces:** Tidy gardens, lawns and pathways, or adding a deck/patio, create a strong first impression and improve lifestyle appeal.

Buying another property

The equity you build in your first home can be used in several ways. Here's a very basic overview so you understand how equity can help you purchase your next property, whether you're buying to live in or investing first.

How to set up borrowing if your next property is an investment

If you're buying your home to live in, it may never become an investment. In most cases, people sell their first home when they buy their second, as the equity they've built is what they need for the next property. For the majority of first-home buyers, the equity in their first property is used in one of three ways:

- *Upsize to a larger home*: use the equity built over three to five years to buy a home that better suits your longer term needs and lifestyle.
- *Renovate or improve the current home*: stay in the property long term, possibly using equity or savings to fund renovations that make the home more suitable.
- *Invest in a second property*: use the equity to fund a property that will be purely for investment purposes.

You might choose to employ one or more of these options but you should focus on what's important to you. Doing one may prevent you from doing another, so it's a good idea to revisit your goals and your 'why' before making a move.

For example, if your 'why' involves upsizing in five years, you may decide not to purchase an investment property in the meantime, as it could affect your ability to achieve that goal. Similarly, if your goal is to use equity to upsize in three to five years, you want to ensure you're not using that equity for other purposes before you need it.

At any stage along your property journey, you can revisit the scenarios you worked through in your strategy and lending discussions with your mortgage broker.

For instance, you might be considering using $50 000 of your usable equity for a renovation. Before committing, it's important to know how much your repayments will be once the renovation is complete. You don't want to start a project without confirming that the repayments will remain comfortably within your budget.

How to use equity in property 1 for property 2

Most people think you need to save a deposit every time you buy a home, but you don't. Your first property does the heavy lifting. It grows quietly in the background, building equity while you live your life. Your 'why' may change with time and your equity will help meet those goals in any form, whether that be renovations, upsizing, investing in property, investing in other assets or even downsizing. See figure 10.1, which demonstrates how equity in property 1 can be used to purchase property 2.

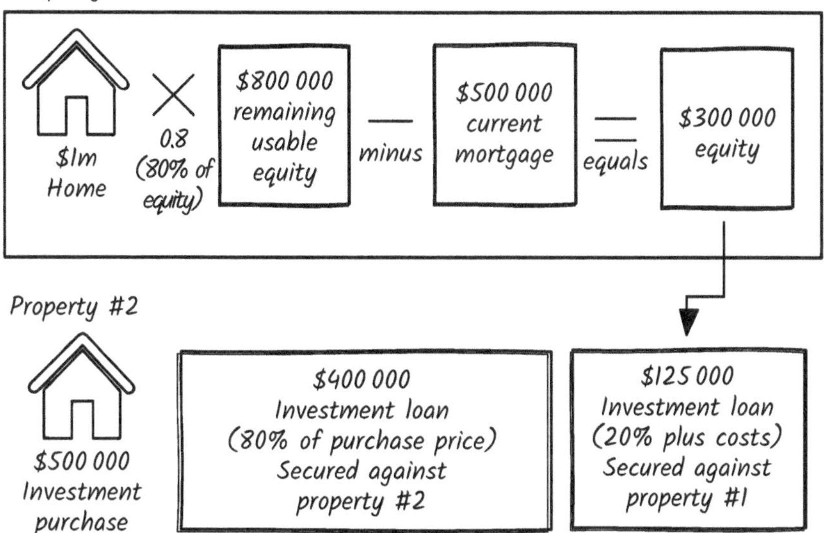

Figure 10.1: using the equity in one property to purchase another one

Figure 10.1 illustrates an existing home loan of $500 000 secured against an owner-occupied property. As the property increases in value, additional equity becomes available, allowing a separate loan split of $125 000 to be created against the home for the deposit and purchasing costs of an investment property. While this split is used solely for investment purposes, it remains secured against the home. The balance of the purchase is funded by a separate $400 000 loan secured only against the new investment property.

Together, the $125 000 and $400 000 loans represent 105 per cent of the investment property purchase price; however, because the loan secured against the investment property itself is only 80 per cent LVR, no LMI is payable. From an accounting perspective, both the $125 000 equity loan and the $400 000 investment loan are treated as tax-deductible debt for the investment and are generally structured as interest-only loans. The only non-tax-deductible debt is the original $500 000 home loan, which is why all offset accounts, including the one receiving rental income, are linked to the home loan and all surplus cash and additional repayments are directed there. This structure keeps securities separate, limits risk to the owner-occupied property and provides flexibility as circumstances change.

The strategy can be repeated for future purchases by creating additional equity splits for deposits and costs, while still maintaining clear loan separation. In a rentvesting scenario, the principle is similar, using equity in one property to purchase another, but as there is no dedicated home loan, all lending is generally tax deductible, with offsets still able to be utilised effectively.

Money, love and relationships

Talk with anyone who has worked in personal finance and they'll say the person you choose to date/marry/partner up with, is one of the most financially significant decisions you'll make. So choose wisely. Cool, let's end the book here.

Just kidding.

Money and relationships get complicated fast. Communication is usually the problem and the solution. We want to quickly touch on how to make money and relationships work, because with property in particular, there are big assets involved and we want you to make the best decisions. And if you have done as we've encouraged you to do in this book, you may have purchased a property before that special someone has walked into your life in a cloud of mist and love hearts. So, these conversations around how assets are managed or dealt with upon moving in or separating are important. Let's protect the wealth you've started building!

Before buying a property together, it's essential to have lots of conversations. What if you get into a relationship after you've started buying properties alone? Many people buy a property before meeting their partner and it's important to discuss how this looks.

Have conversations together around the following:

- Will you be joining finances?
- Are your finances staying separate?
- If someone is moving into a property you own, have you discussed whether they're sharing expenses or contributing to the mortgage? Do you both understand your agreement and are you both on the same page?

Sometimes a binding financial agreement (BFA) is the most appropriate way to put something in place that outlines how finances are to be dealt with during and, if applicable, after the relationship. Most people see a solicitor when ending a relationship, but it can be a great idea to consult one when moving in together.

Having seen many clients separate without any agreement, it's clear how valuable even a simple written agreement can be. Documenting property valuations, savings statements and a list of assets and liabilities at the time of moving in together may not always stand up in court, but it reduces disputes and helps outline 'what ifs' before finances are joined.

A BFA isn't for everyone and life changes like marriage or having children can affect its relevance. But knowing it exists and considering whether it's appropriate is a great starting point for protecting both parties. If you're keen to learn more about BFAs, we have an episode on the *this is property* podcast that can help (ep. 730).

Buying your first property comes with a lot to think about—from choosing the right asset type, understanding title and zoning and weighing up new vs established homes, to managing ongoing costs, renovations and how relationships can impact your finances. Take the time to do your homework, know your goals and plan for both the financial and emotional aspects of property ownership. You've got the tools and knowledge ... now it's time to put them into action. Good luck out there!

Start with this...

Congratulations property owner! Now spend some time on the following:

* Ensure your spending plan or budget are set up and in line with your new property expenses.
* Start setting yourself up for your next move, whether that's releasing a guarantee, adding value to your property or setting a reminder to check your equity position.

What I wish I'd known

Hindsight is a powerful thing. In life, and especially with money and property, it's often only after you've been through the process that the lessons become obvious. The challenge is that we rarely get the benefit of our own hindsight before making big decisions. That's why we asked some survey respondents a simple but important question: *What do you wish you had known when you purchased your first home?*

The responses that you'll find below are anonymous and presented verbatim from our survey. They reflect real experiences by people who have lived through the process, including both the wins and the pain points. Taken together, this list is incredibly valuable, not because it provides one perfect answer, but because it exposes the patterns, blind spots and hard-earned lessons that first-home buyers consistently discover too late.

When you step back and look across these responses, clear themes emerge. Many buyers felt pressured by real estate agents, struggled to know who to trust and were pushed to make decisions faster than they felt comfortable doing. Confusion around pricing, fear of making the wrong offer and frustration with uneven access to information came up repeatedly. Buyers often described feeling overwhelmed, underprepared and unsure whether the advice they were receiving was genuinely in their best interests. For some, this pressure led to regret, particularly where due diligence was skipped, costs were underestimated or emotional decisions were made just to get into the market.

Just as clearly, there were strong patterns around what helped. Time and again, respondents pointed to the value of good mortgage brokers, buyers' agents and conveyancers who acted as calm, experienced guides through a complex process. These professionals helped buyers understand their real borrowing limits and stress-test repayments; navigate auctions and push back when things didn't feel right. Don't just take it from us. These insights come directly from people who have been through it and they reinforce why having the right team, asking better questions and slowing the process down can make the difference between a stressful scramble and a confident, well-informed purchase.

Here we go ...

- I didn't use a conveyancer and felt pressured to sign. I was overwhelmed and wish I had negotiated more.

- I loved inspecting properties, especially furnished ones. It helped me understand space properly. I wish I'd understood earlier that real estate agents can't be trusted and that in a hot market you must chase them.

- I wish there was more focus on whether you can actually manage repayments long term, not just how much you can borrow.

- I hated the whole process. The paperwork was awful. Having a mortgage broker was the only good part.

- I wish I had just used a buyers' agent from the start. I could have bought in a better area.
- As a woman buying on my own, navigating real estate agents was the hardest part. Sexism, assumptions and inappropriate behaviour were constant. My mortgage broker was incredibly empowering and made a huge difference.
- Auctions were made out to be terrifying, but once I did one it was actually transparent and straightforward.
- It was easier than I expected. I wish we had spoken to a broker earlier and not stressed so much about bank statements.
- The biggest shock was how many extra costs there are. Furnishing, cleaning, moving, storage and all the small things add up fast.
- Legal, search, loan and bank fees added thousands we hadn't budgeted for.
- We migrated to Australia and had to learn everything on the fly. It was a great learning experience but very overwhelming.
- I tried to play the agent game but eventually gave up and got a buyer's agent. I wish I'd known earlier about guarantors and lower deposit options.
- I had no idea mortgage brokers would be so involved or that they were free. I wish there were better tools to stress test what we could comfortably afford.
- Making formal offers was exciting and made it feel real. I wish I'd known about low deposit schemes earlier.

- I only thought about mortgage repayments and underestimated all the other ownership costs.
- I went straight to the bank and didn't know mortgage brokers existed. That was a mistake.
- I didn't understand the difference between redraw and offset and thought they were the same.
- Agents defaulted to speaking to my partner even though I was the buyer. It was overwhelming.
- Open homes are fun at first, but they get draining very quickly.
- Using a buyers' agent made everything much less daunting, even though it was still stressful.
- A great mortgage broker made us realise we were much closer to buying than we thought.
- Understanding borrowing power and government schemes earlier would have helped us get in sooner.
- It was far more stressful than expected. It's not just a deposit. We really needed closer to 15 per cent once all costs were included.
- There were so many unknowns and it was hard to know who to trust.
- I should have started earlier and not overthought everything.
- Buying on my own gave me confidence, but the male-dominated nature of the industry was confronting.

- Inspections were exciting and scary. Organising finance and paperwork was overwhelming.
- I wish I had thought about the property as a future investment, not just a home.
- The process is incredibly competitive and emotionally draining when you miss out repeatedly.
- You don't need a 20 per cent deposit, but I didn't know that at the time.
- I loved the research but hated dodgy agents and incorrect contracts.
- Once you find an agent who treats buyers with respect, it changes everything.
- I felt dumb trying to work out whether to offer under, over or at the asking price.
- I wish someone had explained the full timeline from offer to settlement.
- After signing the contract, I felt completely blind about what came next.
- Don't buy a high-rise apartment off the plan. Valuation risk is real.
- I wish I had the confidence to question so-called experts earlier.
- Don't get emotionally attached until the property is unconditional.
- Building our first home was great, but I underestimated the true cost and complexity of building.

- Everything before signing was fine. What happens after signing is the most daunting part.
- I didn't understand where the money actually goes at settlement.
- Not all brokers are good. Comfort and familiarity are not the same as competence.
- I trusted agents too much and didn't do enough due diligence. Good brokers and conveyancers are worth their weight in gold.
- Maintenance costs in the first year nearly caught us out.
- Owning a home felt empowering after renting, but the buying costs were far higher than expected.
- I wish I understood lending mechanics better and how emotions can lead to overpaying.
- There are plenty of properties out there. Don't let agents pressure you.
- Understanding inspection reports and disclosures is critical.

For what it's worth, Rach wishes she had better understood the difference between purchase price and cost to hold. While her first investment property was cheap to buy, it ended up costing her more over the long run due to higher ongoing holding costs than if she had purchased a higher quality asset at a higher price. In hindsight, investing in a stronger property from the outset would have delivered a more sustainable outcome, despite the larger initial purchase price.

Glen wishes he had known that anytime you do something for the first time it comes with some nerves, anxiety and stress, but once you get settled you wish you'd taken a bigger risk!

Our aim with this book is to help make your first property purchase so considered and well informed that when you're later asked what you wish you had known, your answer is simple:

I have no regrets. I trusted myself, took action based on my situation at the time, aligned my decision with my goals and did what I needed to do for that stage of my life.

Good luck with your property purchase. We're here to help; we trust we have already.

Find us on Instagram:

Glen: @moneypodcast.aus
Rach: @rachellekroon_money

For further information, explainer videos, templates and other resources, follow the QR code below:

Or use the URL: investingbook.com.au/firstpropertyresources

Index